Bardell v. Pickw

Bardell v. Pickwick

Percy Fitzgerald

Published by Hesperus Press Limited
28 Mortimer Street, London W1W 7RD
www.hesperuspress.com

First published 1902
First published by Hesperus Press Limited, 2012

Foreword © Baroness Hale, 2012

Designed and typeset by Fraser Muggeridge studio
Printed in Jordan by Jordan National Press

ISBN: 978-1-84391-364-1

CONTENTS

Dickens was no stranger to my county of Richmondshire in the North Riding of Yorkshire. In 1839 he stayed in Greta Bridge, on the road from Scotch Corner to Carlisle, on his way to visit Dotheboys Hall in nearby Bowes. His visit is commemorated in the Dickens Bar of the Morritt Arms – a favourite watering hole then and now – decorated in 1948 by Jack Gilroy with lively murals as a favour to the then owner, an ancestor of the current Chancellor of the High Court, Sir Andrew Morritt. Prominent among the Dickensian figures adorning the walls is Mr Pickwick, dancing a jig without a care in the world, as if the case of *Bardell v. Pickwick* had never happened.

The story of Mr Pickwick and Mrs Bardell is but a small part of the *Posthumous Papers of the Pickwick Club* – indeed the relevant portions of the book are quoted verbatim in Percy Fitzgerald's entertaining commentary on the case, which was tried before a judge and jury at the City of London Guildhall on, of course, April Fool's Day in 1828.

To twenty-first-century eyes everything about the case looks like ancient history. The common law action for breach of promise of marriage was abolished by the Law Reform (Miscellaneous Provisions) Act 1970 (which also abolished the common law action for enticing away a spouse and the husband's action for damages against an adulterer) – as Stephen Cretney comments in *Family Law in the Twentieth Century*, 'Family life was thus further distanced from the world of commercial bargains and property deals'. The right to demand trial by jury in a civil action was mostly abolished by the Administration of Justice (Miscellaneous Provisions) Act 1933, but it was kept for breach of promise of marriage actions until they too were abolished. The inability of the parties to give evidence in support of their own case was abolished by the Evidence Act 1851, probably the most important change between the date of the fictional trial in 1828 and the first publication of Fitzgerald's book in 1902. Imprisonment for debt was largely abolished by the Debtors Act 1869, but this would scarcely have helped Mr Pickwick, who refused to satisfy the judgment debt owing to Mrs Bardell as a matter of principle even though he could afford to do so. He would have had to wait until the Administration of Justice Act 1970 – if other forces had not intervened to save the situation. The Fleet Prison was pulled down in 1846 but the Marshalsea survived until the 1870s.

So, ancient history though *Bardell v. Pickwick* might seem, it is within living memory that a modern Mr Pickwick might be sued for breach of promise of marriage, tried by a jury, and sent to prison for up to six weeks if he pig-headedly failed to pay the damages awarded. Peter Bromley's textbook on *Family Law*, first published in 1957, had a whole chapter devoted to Contracts to Marry, which were very much like any other contract. The sexism of an earlier age creeps in: 'Although it is customary for a man not to sue the woman for breach of promise, there is clearly no difference in law whether the promisee be the man or the woman and either may sue the other'. So it was thought that marriage was more valuable to a woman than to a man, or possibly that only a cad would keep a woman to her word, or possibly that most women were not worth suing for damages (damages being the only remedy, as equity obviously would not grant specific performance to force them to marry). Unlike an ordinary contract, however, Mr Pickwick would have had a defence if he could have shown that Mrs Bardell was suffering from some moral, physical or mental infirmity rendering her unfit for marriage which he had discovered after the engagement: '... the plaintiff's unchastity (at least if she be a woman), impotence or insanity would be a good defence, but not that she does not have the income that the defendant thought that she had...'; the sexual double standard survived until 1970.

But Mr Pickwick's defence was not that Mrs Bardell was unfit for marriage – she plainly was not – but that he had never offered to marry her at all. And this is the most curious feature of Fitzgerald's account. The modern contract lawyer would want to know precisely what words or conduct were alleged to constitute the proposal in question and consider whether, objectively understood in their context, they amounted to a contractual offer. The principal witnesses to the crucial conversation were Mr Pickwick and Mrs Bardell, who could not give evidence at the trial in 1828. No doubt this is why Fitzgerald does not quote the passage from the book, which relates that conversation, until he gets to the trial (see pp. 62–5). Instead he begins (see pp. 9–10) with the dramatic scene which confronted the Pickwickians that unlucky morning in July 1827, when they surprised Mr Pickwick with his landlady fainting in his arms in a hysterical condition. But what had led up to it?

The modern lawyer would not wait until the trial and the evidence of what Mrs Cluppins might have heard through the door which was 'on the jar'. The modern lawyer would start with the parties' own evidence of their conversation. So we shall give you now the author's account of the conversation on which the action is based. Mrs Cluppins was probably not a reliable historian or a neutral observer, but we must assume that Dickens has told us the truth about the conversation. Picture to yourselves, therefore, the scene described in Chapter XII: 'Descriptive of a Very Important Proceeding on the Part of Mr Pickwick; no less an epoch in his life, than in this History'.

To anyone acquainted with... the domestic economy of the establishment, and conversant with the admirable regulation of Mr Pickwick's mind, his appearance and behaviour on the morning... would have been most mysterious and unaccountable. He paced the room to and fro with hurried steps, popped his head out of the window at intervals of about three minutes each, constantly referred to his watch, and exhibited many other manifestations of impatience very unusual with him. It was evident that something of great importance was in contemplation, but what that something was, not even Mrs Bardell herself had been enabled to discover.

'Mrs Bardell,' said Mr Pickwick, at last, as that amiable female approached the termination of a prolonged dusting of the apartment.

'Sir,' said Mrs Bardell.

'Your little boy is a very long time gone.'

'Why it's a good long way to the Borough, sir,' remonstrated Mrs Bardell.

'Ah,' said Mr Pickwick, 'very true; so it is.'

Mr Pickwick relapsed into silence, and Mrs Bardell resumed her dusting.

'Mrs Bardell,' said Mr Pickwick, at the expiration of a few minutes.

'Sir,' said Mrs Bardell again.

'Do you think it a much greater expense to keep two people, than to keep one?'

'La, Mr Pickwick,' said Mrs Bardell, colouring up to the very border of her cap, as she fancied she observed a species of matrimonial twinkle in the eyes of her lodger; 'La, Mr Pickwick, what a question!'

'Well, but *do* you?' inquired Mr Pickwick.

'That depends –' said Mrs Bardell, approaching the duster very near to Mr Pickwick's elbow, which was planted on the table – 'that depends a good deal upon the person, you know, Mr Pickwick; and whether it's a saving and careful person, sir.'

'That's very true,' said Mr Pickwick, 'but the person I have in my eye (here he looked very hard at Mrs Bardell) I think possesses those qualities; and has, moreover, a considerable knowledge of the world, and a great deal of sharpness, Mrs Bardell, which may be of material use to me.'

'La, Mr Pickwick,' said Mrs Bardell; the crimson rising to her cap-border again.

'I do,' said Mr Pickwick, growing energetic, as was his wont in speaking of a subject which interested him, 'I do, indeed; and to tell you the truth, Mrs Bardell, I have made up my mind.'

'Dear me, sir,' exclaimed Mrs Bardell.

'You'll think it very strange now,' said the amiable Mr Pickwick with a good-humoured glance at his companion, 'that I never consulted you about this matter, and never even mentioned it, till I sent your little boy out this morning – eh?'

Mrs Bardell could only reply by a look. She had long worshipped Mr Pickwick at a distance, but here she was, all at once, raised to a pinnacle to which her wildest and most extravagant hopes had never dared to aspire. Mr Pickwick was going to propose – a deliberate plan, too – sent her little boy to the Borough, to get him out of the way – how thoughtful – how considerate!

'Well,' said Mr Pickwick, 'what do you think?'

'Oh, Mr Pickwick,' said Mrs Bardell, trembling with agitation, 'you're very kind, sir.'

'It'll save you a good deal of trouble, won't it,' said Mr Pickwick.

'Oh, I never thought anything of the trouble, sir,' replied Mrs Bardell; 'and, of course, I should take more trouble to please you than ever; but it is so kind of you, Mr Pickwick, to have so much consideration for my loneliness.'

'Ah, to be sure,' said Mr Pickwick; 'I never thought of that. When I am in town, you'll always have somebody to sit with you. To be sure, so you will.'

'I'm sure I ought to be a very happy woman,' said Mrs Bardell.

'And your little boy –' said Mr Pickwick.

'Bless his heart!' interposed Mrs Bardell, with a maternal sob.

'He, too, will have a companion,' resumed Mr Pickwick, 'a lively one, who'll teach him, I'll be bound, more tricks in a week than he would ever learn in a year.' And Mr Pickwick smiled placidly.

'Oh you dear –' said Mrs Bardell.

Mr Pickwick started.

'Oh you good, kind, playful dear,' said Mrs Bardell; and without more ado, she rose from her chair, and flung her arms round Mr Pickwick's neck, with a cataract of tears and a chorus of sobs.

'Bless my soul,' cried the astonished Mr Pickwick; – 'Mrs Bardell my good woman – dear me, what a situation – pray consider – Mrs Bardell, don't – if anybody should come –'

'Oh, let them come,' exclaimed Mrs Bardell, frantically; 'I'll never leave you – dear, kind, good, soul;' and, with these words, Mrs Bardell clung the tighter.

'Mercy upon me,' said Mr Pickwick, struggling violently, 'I hear somebody coming up the stairs. Don't, don't, there's a good creature, don't.' But entreaty and remonstrance were alike unavailing: for Mrs Bardell had fainted in Pickwick's arms; and before he could gain time to deposit her in a chair, Master Bardell entered the room, ushering in Mr Tupman, Mr Winkle, and Mr Snodgrass.

Suppose for a moment that the parties' evidence does not materially differ (and there is always the unsatisfactory Mrs Cluppins in support). Members of the jury, what is your verdict? Subjectively, of course, as the reader knows, Mr Pickwick was thinking of hiring Sam Weller as his manservant. Objectively, however, would a neutral observer reasonably have understood him to have made an offer of marriage which Mrs Bardell had accepted before he hastened to correct the impression he had given? As Fitzgerald comments, 'It must be said the impression of a listener, who has heard all this, could have been anything but favourable to Mr Pickwick' (p. 05).

Boz himself comments in his Preface that Mr Pickwick becomes more good and more sensible as the book proceeds – and this is not surprising, because in real life 'the peculiarities and oddities of a man who has anything whimsical about him, generally impress us first, and it is not until we are better acquainted with him that we usually begin to look below these superficial traits, and to know the better part of him'. Judge for yourselves, dear readers, from Percy Fitzgerald's entertaining and instructive account of what happened next, whether Mr Pickwick did indeed become more sensible in his dealings in the action of *Bardell v. Pickwick*...

– *Baroness Hale of Richmond, 2012*
Justice of the Supreme Court of the United Kingdom

Bardell v. Pickwick

The trial for breach of promise of marriage held at the Guildhall sittings, on 1st April 1828, before Mr Justice Stareleigh and a Special Jury of the city of London.

There are few things more familiar or more interesting to the public than this *cause célèbre*. It is better known than many a real case: for everyone knows the judge, his name and remarks – also the counsel – (notably Serjeant Buzfuz) – the witnesses, and what they said – and of course all about the plaintiff and the famous defendant. It was tried over seventy years ago at 'the Guildhall Settens', and was described by Boz some sixty-three years ago. Yet every detail seems fresh – and as fresh as ever. It is astonishing that a purely technical sketch like this, whose humours might be relished only by such specialists as barristers and attorneys, who would understand the jokes levelled at the profession, should be so well understood of the people. All see the point of the legal satire. It is quite a prodigy. Boz had the art, in an extraordinary degree, of thus vividly commending trade processes, professional allusions, and methods to outsiders, and making them humorous and intelligible. Witness Jackson, when he came to 'serve' Mr Pickwick and friend with the *subpoenas*. It is a dry, business-like process, but how racy Boz made it. A joke sparkles in every line.

This trial for breach has been debated over and over again among lawyers and barristers, some contending that 'there was no evidence at all to go to the jury' as to a promise; others insisting on misdirection, and that there was evidence that ought not to have been admitted. The law has since been changed, and by later Acts both Mrs Bardell and Mr Pickwick would have been allowed to tell their stories and to have been cross-examined. Mrs Bardell was almost justified in suspecting that Mr Pickwick was offering his hand when he was merely speaking of engaging a manservant. But then the whole would have been spoiled. Under the present systems, this would all have come out. Mr Pickwick, when it came to his turn, would have explained what his proceedings meant. It is a most perfect and vivid satire on the hackneyed methods of the lawyers when dealing with the witnesses. Nothing can be more natural or more graphic. It is maintained to something between the level of comedy and farce: nor is there the least exaggeration. It applies now as it did then, though not to the same topics. A hectoring, bullying counsel, threatening and cruel, would interfere with the pleasant tone of the play; but it is all the same conveyed. There is a likeness to Bardell v. Pickwick in another burlesque case, tried in our day, the well-known 'Trial by Jury', the joint work of Mr Gilbert and the late Sir Arthur Sullivan. The general tone of both is the same and in the modern work there is a general Pickwickian flavour. Sir Arthur's music, too, is highly 'Pickwickian', and the joint effort of the two humorists is infinitely diverting. The judge is something of a Stareleigh.

The truth is that Boz, the engenderer of these facetiae, apart from his literary gift, was one of the most brilliant, capable young fellows of his generation. Whatever he did, he did in the best way, and in the brightest way. But his power of obser-vation and of seeing what might be termed the humorous quiddity of anything, was extraordinary.

To put absurdity in a proper view for satirical purposes, it has to be generalised from a number of instances, familiar to all. Those legal oddities, the public has seen over and over again, but they had passed unnoticed till this clever observer set to work and noted them. As I say, it requires a deep know-ledge of the law to set these things in a grotesque light.

Boz had been a sort of general reporter on the *Chronicle*: he 'took' everything. He had reported at police courts as well as at the law courts. His quick and bright intelligence seized the humours here, as it did those of the street. He later reported in the gallery, and was dispatched across the country in post-chaises to 'take' eminent political speakers – always winning the hearty commendation of his employers for his zeal and energy.

Mr Pickwick was a well-to-do bachelor, who lived by himself near the city, where he had been in trade. His age was about fifty, as can be accurately calculated by his remark on the sliding at Manor Farm. 'I used to do so on the gutters when I was a boy... but I haven't done such a thing these thirty years.' This was said in 1828. He resided in Goswell Street – now Goswell Road – with a widow lady, whose husband had been in the Excise. He cannot have paid more than a pound a week, if so much, for two rooms on the first floor. There was no servant, and the hardworking landlady, Mrs Martha Bardell, performed all the duties of her household single-handed. As her counsel later described it – and see all she did for him! – 'She waited on him, attended to his comforts, cooked his meals, looked out his linen for the washer-woman when it went abroad, darned, aired, and prepared it for his wear when it came home, and, in short, enjoyed his fullest trust and confidence.' This Serjeant Buzfuz, duly 'instructed'. Not only was there Mr Pickwick, but there was another lodger, and her little boy Tommy. The worthy woman took care of and looked after all three. This might incline us to take a favourable view of her. She regarded her lodger with feelings of veneration and attachment, of which proof is found in her later talk with Sam. To him she said that 'he had always behaved himself like a perfect gentleman' and then added this significant speech: 'It's a terrible thing to be dragged in this way before the public, but *I now see* that it's the only thing that I ought to do.' That is, she seems to have held out as long as possible, believing that her amiable lodger would act as a perfect gentleman and like himself. But when she found that even an action had no terrors for him, she saw that there was nothing else to do but to let the action go on.

And what was Mrs Bardell like? One would imagine her a plump, buxom widow, 'fat, fair and forty', with her dear little boy, 'the only pledge of her deceased exciseman', or say something between thirty and forty years old. Fortunately, two portraits have come down to us of the lady – one somewhat of this pattern and depicting her, as she flung herself on Mr Pickwick on the disastrous morning: the other – a swollen, dreadful thing, which must be a caricature of the literal present-ment. Here we see a woman of gross, enormous proportions seated on the front bench and apparently weighing some thirteen or fourteen stone, with a vast coarse face. This is surely an unfair presentment of the worthy landlady; besides, Dodson and Fogg were too astute practitioners to imperil their chances by exhibiting to his Lordship and the Jury so ill-favoured a plaintiff. Indeed, we are told that they arranged a rather theatrical exhibition in this scene, with a view of creating an impression in their favour.

Many find pleasure in reading the Booksellers Catalogues, and a vast number are showered on me in the course of the year. But on one of these I always gaze with special interest, and even tenderness. For it comes from one Herbert, who lives in Goswell Road. Only think, *Goswell* Road – erst Goswell Street, where just seventy years ago Mrs Bardell was letting lodgings and Mr Pickwick himself was lodging: and on the cover I read, a further attraction, 'Goswell Road, near "The Angel"', whence the 'stage' which took the party to the 'Spaniard' at Hampstead started! Sometimes I am drawn to the shop, crowded with books; but one's thoughts stray away from the books into speculations as to *which* house it was. But the indications are most vague, though the eye settles on a decent range of shabby-looking faded tenements – two storeys high only – and which *look* like lodging-houses. Some ingenious commentators have indeed ventured to identify the house itself, arguing from the very general description in the text.

We should note, however, Mr Pickwick's lack of caution. He came in the very next day, having apparently made no enquiries as to the landlady. Had he done so, he would have learned of the drunken exciseman who met his death by being knocked on the head with a quart pot. He might have heard of the friends, Cluppins, Raddle, etc., who seemed to have been charwomen or something of the sort; also that there was a sort of working man as a fellow lodger. Above all, that there was no servant in the house. All which boded ill, and made it likely that Mr Pickwick would be the easy victim of some crafty scheme.

All went well until the unlucky morning in July 1827, when Mr Pickwick's friends, coming to pay a morning call, and entering unexpectedly, surprised Mr Pickwick with his landlady fainting in his arms in a hysterical condition. This was a very awkward business. The delinquent, however, did not at once grasp the situation, and could not 'make head or tail of it, or what the lady meant'. His friends, however, had their doubts:

'What is the matter?' said the three tongue-tied Pick-wickians.

'I don't know,' replied Mr Pickwick, pettishly. 'Now, help me, lead this woman downstairs.'

'Oh, I am better now,' said Mrs Bardell, faintly.

'Let me lead you downstairs,' said the ever gallant Mr Tupman.

'Thank you, sir – thank you,' exclaimed Mrs Bardell, hysterically. And downstairs she was led accordingly, accompanied by her affectionate son.

'I cannot conceive –' said Mr Pickwick, when his friend returned – 'I cannot conceive what has been the matter with that woman. I had merely announced to her my intention of keeping a manservant, when she fell into the extraordinary paroxysm in which you found her. Very extraordinary thing.'

'Very,' said his three friends.

'Placed me in such an extremely awkward situation,' continued Mr Pickwick.

'Very,' was the reply of his followers, as they coughed slightly, and looked dubiously at each other.

This behaviour was not lost upon Mr Pickwick. He remarked their incredulity. They evidently suspected him.

It may be reasonably supposed that Mr Pickwick had not been very discreet, or sufficiently cautious in his general behaviour to his landlady. As we know, he was rather too effusive in his relations with the fair sex. One of his weaknesses was *kissing*. He would kiss everybody who was young or good-looking. His maxim was 'Kiss early and kiss often.' Who can forget his *systematic* method of greeting the engaging Arabella? 'He (1) took off his spectacles, (2) in great haste, and (3) taking both the young lady's hands in his (4) kissed her (5) a great many times (6) perhaps a greater number of times than was absolutely necessary.' Old rogue! I have little doubt that on his return home from his tours he encircled the buxom figure of Mrs Bardell – all of course in his own paternal and privileged way.

It should be borne in mind also that Mr Pickwick was almost invariably drawn into his more serious scrapes and embarrassment by this devotion to the sex. The night in the boarding school garden   the affair with the top spinster lady – his interview with Arabella from the top of the wall – his devotion to Mrs Pott and Mrs Dowler – and much more that we do not hear of, show that he was a gallant elderly gentleman. Oh he was a 'sly dog, he was'.

There is a curious burst of Mr Pickwick's which seems to hint at a sort of tender appreciation on his side. When the notice of trial was sent to him, in his first vehemence, he broke out that Mrs Bardell had nothing to do with the business, 'She hadn't the heart to do it.' Mr Pickwick could not speak with this certainty, unless he knew the lady's feelings pretty well. *Why* hadn't she the heart to do it? Because she was sincerely attached to him and his interests and was 'a dear creature'. This, however, was a fond delusion of the worthy gentleman's. Persons of her class are not quite so disinterested as they appear to be, especially if they have to interpret the various paternal and comforting advances made to them by their well-to-do lodgers.

There is another factor which can hardly be left out, when considering Mr Pickwick's responsibility – that is, his too frequent indulgence in liquor, and the insufficiency of his head to stand its influence. Now this was a very important day for him, the first he was to set up a manservant. He had to break it to his landlady, who would naturally resent the change. He may have been *priming* himself with some of those perpetual glasses of brandy and water to which he was addicted, and who knows but that, in his ardour to propitiate, he may have gone a *little* too far? This fact too, of the introducing a manservant into her establishment, Mrs Bardell may have indistinctly associated with a general change in his life. If she were to become Mrs Pickwick her duties might be naturally expected to devolve on a male assistant.

Next morning he and his friends quitted London on their travels to Eatenswill in pursuit of adventure. He airily dismissed the matter. We may wonder whether he made any remonstrance to his landlady before his departure. Probably he did not, fancying that she had merely had a slight fit of the 'tantrums'.

At Bury, however, after the boarding-school adventure, he was to be painfully awakened. He was sitting with his friends after dinner at the 'Angel', in his happiest mood. Winkle had related his quarrel with Pott *in re* Mrs Pott, in a humorous fashion when one of the most delightful of humorous scenes followed.

Mr Pickwick was proceeding with his scathing rebuke, when Sam enters with a letter.

'I don't know this hand,' said Mr Pickwick, opening the letter. 'Mercy on us! What's this? It must be a jest; it – it – can't be true.'

'What's the matter?' was the general inquiry.

'Nobody dead, is there?' said Wardle, alarmed at the horror in Mr Pickwick's countenance.

Mr Pickwick made no reply but pushing the letter across the table, and desiring Mr Tupman to read it aloud, fell back in his chair with a look of vacant astonishment quite alarming to behold.

Mr Tupman, with a trembling voice, read the letter, of which the following is a copy:

Freeman's Court, Cornhill, August 28th, 1827.
Bardell against Pickwick.
Sir,
Have been instructed by Mrs Martha Bardell to commence an action against you for a breach of promise of marriage, for which the plaintiff lays her damage at fifteen hundred pounds, we beg to inform you that a writ has been issued

against you in this suit of the Court of Common Pleas;
and request to know, by return of post, the name of your
attorney in London, who will accept service thereof.

We are, Sir,
Your obedient servants
Dodson & Fogg
Mr Samuel Pickwick

So Mr Pickwick, the general mentor, the philosopher and friend – the man of high moral tone, 'born to set the world aright' – the general lecturer of his 'followers', was now in for an action at law of the most awkward and unpleasant kind. To be philandering with one's landlady! Rather low form this. But what would they say down at Manor Farm? How Isabelle Wardle and her sister – and all the girls – would laugh! And the spinster aunt – *she* would enjoy it! But there was no help for it. It must be faced.

Naturally Mr Pickwick felt uncomfortable, and his first idea was to arrange the matter. This was a sensible course, and he ought at once to have put the matter into the hands of his friend Perker, with full powers to treat. But no. Mr Pickwick's vanity and indiscretion made him meddle in the business behind his solicitor's back, as it were, and with damaging results to himself – a warning to all such amateurs. It must be said that Dodson and Fogg's behaviour at the extraordinary visit which he paid them was marked by a certain propriety. Mr Pickwick insisted on knowing what were the grounds of action – that is, the details of the evidence against him – in short, their case. They, very correctly, refused to tell him. 'The case may be false or it may be true – it may be credible it may be incredible.' But all the same it was a strong case. This was as much as they could tell. Mr Pickwick could only urge that if 'it were so, he was a most unfortunate man', on which Dodson promptly – 'I hope you are, sir, I trust you may be, sir. If you are really innocent, you are more unfortunate than I had believed any man could possibly be.'

Mr Pickwick then rather foolishly asked did he understand they meant to go on with the action – as if they could have been affected by his declaration. 'Understand?' was the reply, 'that you certainly may' – a very natural speech.

With some want of professional delicacy and etiquette, Dodson seized the opportunity to 'serve' Mr Pickwick; but they were not a high-class firm and their methods were not high-class. Then an extraordinarily incredible display followed. His passion broke forth. 'Of all the disgraceful and rascally proceedings he ever, etc.!' Dodson summoned his clerks to listen to this gross language, and said, 'Perhaps you would like to call us swindlers.' 'You are,' said Mr Pickwick. Fogg even wished him to assault them – and perhaps he would have done so, but for Sam, who at last got him away. This was certainly not correct, but how aggravated was Mr Pickwick! One is rather astonished at the forbearance of this sharp firm.

Now, had Mr Pickwick gone straight to his lodgings in Goswell Street and seen Mrs Bardell, heard her views and claims, had he been told by her that she had been professionally urged to go to law as she had such a strong case – there might have been some excuse for his violence to Dodson and Fogg. But he knew nothing whatever of the matter – knew nothing of the attorneys – and in his blind fury gratuitously assumed that they had 'conspired' to harass him in this way. True, he had overheard how they had treated poor Ramsey.

This very *malapropos* visit of Mr Pickwick to the firm was, as I said, a mistake and damaged his case. It showed that he was nervous and anxious, and *insecure*. He took nothing by it.

There was in truth much short-sighted cunning in his ways, which came of his overweening vanity. But this was only one of several attempts he made to worm out something to his own advantage.

Another of Mr Pickwick's foolish manoeuvres was his sending his man to his old lodgings to his landlady – ostensibly to fetch away his 'things', when this dialogue passed:

'Tell Mrs Bardell she may put a bill up, as soon as she likes.'

'Wery good, sir,' replied Mr Weller; 'anythin' more, sir?'

'Nothing more, Sam.'

Mr Weller stepped slowly to the door, as if he expected something more; slowly opened it, slowly stepped out, and had slowly closed it within a couple of inches, when Mr Pickwick called out.

'Sam.'

'Sir,' said Mr Weller, stepping quickly back, and closing the door behind him.

'I have no objection, Sam, to your endeavouring to ascertain how Mrs Bardell herself seems disposed towards me, and whether it is really probable that this vile and groundless action is to be carried to extremity. *I say, I do not object to your doing this, if you wish it, Sam,*' said Mr Pickwick. Sam gave a short nod of intelligence and left the room.

Now this was very artful on the part of Mr Pickwick, but it was a very shallow sort of artfulness, and it was later to recoil on himself. Sam of course saw through it at once. It never dawned on this simple-minded man what use the plaintiff's solicitors would make of his *démarche*.

When the subpoenas were served he rushed off to Perker:

'They have subpoena'd my servant too,' said Mr Pickwick.

'Sam?' said Perker.

Mr Pickwick replied in the affirmative.

'Of course, my dear sir, of course. I knew they would. I could have told *you* that a month ago. You know, my dear sir, if you *will* take the management of your affairs into your own hands after intrusting them to your solicitor, you must also take the consequences.' Here Mr Perker drew himself up with conscious dignity, and brushed some stray grains of snuff from his shirt frill.

'And what do they want him to prove?' asked Mr Pickwick, after two or three minutes' silence.

'That you sent him up to the plaintiff's to make some offer of a compromise, I suppose,' replied Perker. 'It don't matter much, though; I don't think many counsel could get a great deal out of *him*.'

'I don't think they could,' said Mr Pickwick.

The minutiae of legal process are prosaic and uninteresting, and it might seem impossible to invest them with any dramatic interest; but how admirably has Boz lighted up and coloured the simple incident of an attorney's clerk – a common, vulgar fellow, of the lowest type, arriving to serve his subpoenas on the witnesses – all assumed to be hostile. The scene is full of touches of light comedy.

'How de do, sir?' said Mr Jackson, nodding to Mr Pickwick.

The gentleman bowed, and looked somewhat surprised for the physiognomy of Mr Jackson dwelt not in his recollection.

'I have called from Dodson and Fogg's,' said Mr Jackson, in an explanatory tone.

Mr Pickwick roused at the name. 'I refer you to my attorney, Sir: Mr Perker, of Gray's Inn,' said he. 'Waiter, show this gentleman out.'

'Beg your pardon, Mr Pickwick,' said Jackson, deliberately depositing his hat on the floor, and drawing from his pocket the strip of parchment. 'But personal service, by clerk of agent, in these cases, you know, Mr Pickwick – nothing like caution, sir, in all legal forms?'

Here Mr Jackson cast his eye on the parchment; and, resting his hands on the table, and looking round with a winning and persuasive smile, said: 'Now, come; don't let's have no words about such a little matter as this. Which of you gentlemen's name's Snodgrass?'

At this enquiry Mr Snodgrass gave such a very undisguised and palpable start, that no further reply was needed.

'Ah! I thought so,' said Mr Jackson, more affably than before. 'I've got a little something to trouble you with, sir.'

'Me!' exclaimed Mr Snodgrass.

'It's only a *subpoena* in Bardell and Pickwick on behalf of the plaintiff,' replied Jackson, singling out one of the slips of paper, and producing a shilling from his waistcoat pocket. 'It'll come on, in the settens after Term; fourteenth of Febrooary, we expect; we've marked it a special jury cause, and it's only ten down the paper. That's yours, Mr Snodgrass.' As Jackson said this he presented the parchment before the eyes of Mr Snodgrass, and slipped the paper and shilling into his hand.

Mr Tupman had witnessed this process in silent astonishment, when Jackson, turning sharply upon him, said: 'I think I ain't mistaken when I say your name's Tupman, am I?'

Mr Tupman looked at Mr Pickwick; but, perceiving no encouragement in that gentleman's widely opened eyes to deny his name, said: 'Yes, my name *is* Tupman, sir.'

'And that other gentleman's Mr Winkle, I think?' said Jackson.

Mr Winkle faltered out a reply in the affirmative; and both gentlemen were forthwith invested with a slip of paper, and a shilling each, by the dextrous Mr Jackson.

'Now,' said Jackson, 'I'm afraid you'll think me rather troublesome, but I want somebody else, if it ain't inconvenient. I *have* Samuel Weller's name here, Mr Pickwick.'

'Send my servant here, waiter,' said Mr Pickwick.

The waiter retired, considerably astonished, and Mr Pickwick motioned Jackson to a seat.

There was a painful pause, which was at length broken by the innocent defendant. 'I suppose, Sir,' said Mr Pickwick, his indignation rising while he spoke; 'I suppose, Sir, that it is the intention of your employers to seek to incriminate me upon the testimony of my own friends?'

Mr Jackson struck his forefinger several times against the left side of his nose, to intimate that he was not there to disclose the secrets of the prison house, and playfully rejoined – 'Not knowin', can't say.'

'For what other reason, Sir,' pursued Mr Pickwick, 'are these subpoenas served upon them, if not for this?'

'Very good plant, Mr Pickwick,' replied Jackson, slowly shaking his head. 'But it won't do. No harm in trying, but there's little to be got out of me.'

Here Mr Jackson smiled once more upon the company, and, applying his left thumb to the tip of his nose, worked a visionary coffee-mill with his right hand, thereby performing a very graceful piece of pantomime (then much in vogue, but now, unhappily, almost obsolete) which was familiarly denominated 'taking a grinder'. [Imagine a modern solicitor's clerk 'taking a grinder!']

'No, no, Mr Pickwick,' said Jackson, in conclusion; 'Perker's people must guess what we've served these sub-poenas for. If they can't, they must wait till the action comes on, and then they'll find out.'

Mr Pickwick bestowed a look of excessive disgust on his unwelcome visitor, and would probably have hurled some tremendous anathema at the heads of Messrs Dodson and Fogg, had not Sam's entrance at the instant inter-rupted him.

'Samuel Weller?' said Mr Jackson, inquiringly.

'Vun o' the truest things as you've said for many a long year,' replied Sam, in a most composed manner.

'Here's a subpoena for you, Mr Weller,' said Jackson.

'What's that in English?' inquired Sam.

'Here's the original,' said Jackson, declining the required explanation.

'Which?' said Sam.

'This,' replied Jackson, shaking the parchment.

'Oh, that's the 'rig'nal, is it?' said Sam. 'Well, I'm wery glad I've seen the 'rig'nal, 'cos it's a gratifyin' sort o' thing, and eases vun's mind so much.'

'And here's the shilling,' said Jackson. 'It's from Dodson and Fogg's.'

'And it's uncommon handsome o' Dodson and Fogg, as knows so little of me, to come down vith a present,' said Sam. 'I feel it as a wery high compliment, sir; it's a wery honourable thing to them, as they knows how to reward merit werever they meets it. Besides which, it's affectin' to one's feelin's.'

As Mr Weller said this, he inflicted a little friction on his right eyelid, with the sleeve of his coat, after the most approved manner of actors when they are in domestic pathetics.

Mr Jackson seemed rather puzzled by Sam's proceedings; but, as he had served the subpoenas, and had nothing more to say, he made a feint of putting on the one glove which he usually carried in his hand, for the sake of appearances; and returned to the office to report progress.

Another of Mr Pickwick's foolish and self-willed proceedings was the interview with Serjeant Snubbin, which he so positively insisted upon. We may wonder nowadays would any K.C. of position have condescended to allow such a proceeding? I fancy it would be thought 'irregular': though perhaps *ex gratia*, and from the oddity of the proposal, it might be conceded.

When Mr Pickwick called upon him, it turned out that the Serjeant knew nothing whatever of his case; probably cared nothing about it. It was not in his line. He perhaps wondered why the old-fashioned lawyer had 'retained' him. We learn Perker's reason:

'Well, we've done everything that's necessary. I have retained Serjeant Snubbin.'

'Is he a good man?' inquired Mr Pickwick.

'Good man!' replied Perker; 'bless your heart and soul, my dear Sir, Serjeant Snubbin is at the very top of his profession. Gets treble the business of any man in court – engaged in every case. You needn't mention it abroad; but we say – we of the profession – that Serjeant Snubbin leads the court by the nose.'

How foolish was this reasoning can be seen on an instant's reflection. To 'lead the court by the nose' is well enough in an argument before a judge: but here it was more important to lead *a jury* by the nose, which Buzfuz knew how to do. Moreover when a counsel has had this power, it usually operates on a special judge and his colleagues; but who could guarantee that Snubbin's special judge would try the case. He as it proved was anything but 'led by the nose'. Perker indeed, summed up the whole weakness of the case in a single sentence:

'They have subpoenaed my three friends,' said Mr Pickwick.

'Ah! of course they would,' replied Perker. 'Important witnesses; saw you in a delicate situation.'

'But she fainted of her own accord,' said Mr Pickwick. 'She threw herself into my arms.'

'Very likely, my dear Sir,' replied Perker; 'very likely and very natural. Nothing more so, my dear Sir, nothing. *But who's to prove it?*'

A suggestion, we are told, that rather 'staggered' Mr Pickwick.

Within ten minutes after he had received reassurance that the thing was impossible, he was conducted by his solicitors into the outer office of the great Serjeant Snubbin himself.

It was an uncarpeted room of tolerable dimensions, with a large writing table drawn up near the fire, the baize top of which had long since lost all claim to its original hue of green, and had gradually grown grey with dust and age, except where all traces of its natural colour were obliterated by ink-stains. Upon the table were numerous little bundles of papers tied with red tape; and behind it, sat an elderly clerk, whose sleek appearance and heavy gold watch-chain presented imposing indications of the extensive and lucrative practice of Mr Serjeant Snubbin.

'Is the Serjeant in his room, Mr Mallard?' inquired Perker, offering his box with all imaginable courtesy.

'Yes, he is,' was the reply, 'but he's very busy. Look here; not an opinion given yet, on any one of these cases; and an expedition fee paid with all of 'em.' The clerk smiled as he said this, and inhaled the pinch of snuff with a zest which seemed to be compounded of a fondness for snuff and a relish for fees.

'Something like practice that,' said Perker.

'Yes,' said the barrister's clerk, producing his own box, and offering it with the greatest cordiality; 'and the best of it is, that as nobody alive except myself can read the Serjeant's writing, they are obliged to wait for the opinions, when he has given them, till I have copied 'em, ha-ha-ha!'

'Which makes good for we know who, besides the Serjeant, and draws a little more out of the clients, eh?' said Perker; 'Ha, ha, ha!' At this the Serjeant's clerk laughed again not a noisy boisterous laugh, but a silent, internal chuckle, which Mr Pickwick disliked to hear. When a man bleeds inwardly, it is a dangerous thing for himself; but when he laughs inwardly, it bodes no good to other people.

'You haven't made me out that little list of the fees that I'm in your debt, have you?' said Perker.

'No, I have not,' replied the clerk.

'I wish you would,' said Perker. 'Let me have them, and I'll send you a cheque. But I suppose you're too busy pocketing the ready money, to think of the debtors, eh? ha, ha, ha!' This sally seemed to tickle the clerk amazingly, and he once more enjoyed a little quiet laugh to himself.

'But, Mr Mallard, my dear friend,' said Perker, suddenly recovering his gravity, and drawing the great man's great man into a corner, by the lappel of his coat; 'you must persuade the Serjeant to see me, and my client here.'

'Come, come,' said the clerk, 'that's not bad either. See the Serjeant! come, that's too absurd.' Notwithstanding the absurdity of the proposal, however, the clerk allowed himself to be gently drawn beyond the hearing of Mr Pickwick; and after a short conversation conducted in whispers, walked softly down a little dark passage, and disappeared into the legal luminary's sanctum, whence he shortly returned on tiptoe, and informed Mr Perker and Mr Pickwick that the Serjeant had been prevailed upon, in violation of all established rules and customs, to admit them at once.

The Serjeant was writing when his clients entered; he bowed abstractedly when Mr Pickwick was introduced by his solicitor; and then, motioning them to a seat, put his pen carefully in the inkstand, nursed his left leg, and waited to be spoken to.

'Mr Pickwick is the defendant in Bardell and Pickwick, Serjeant Snubbin,' said Perker.

'I am retained in that, am I?' said the Serjeant.

'You are, Sir, replied Perker.

The Serjeant nodded his head, and waited for something else.

'Mr Pickwick was anxious to call upon you, Serjeant Snubbin,' said Perker, 'to state to you, before you entered upon the case, that he denies there being any ground or pretence whatever for the action against him; and that unless he came into court with clean hands, and without the most conscientious conviction that he was right in resisting the plaintiff's demand, he would not be there at all. I believe I state your views correctly; do I not, my dear Sir?' said the little man, turning to Mr Pickwick.

'Quite so,' replied that gentleman.

Mr Serjeant Snubbin unfolded his glasses, raised them to his eyes; and, after looking at Mr Pickwick for a few seconds with great curiosity, turned to Mr Perker, and said, smiling slightly as he spoke –

'Has Mr Pickwick a strong case?'

The attorney shrugged his shoulders.

'Do you propose calling witnesses?'

'No.'

The smile on the Serjeant's countenance became more defined; he rocked his leg with increased violence; and, throwing himself back in his easy-chair, coughed dubiously.

These tokens of the Serjeant's presentiments on the subject, slight as they were, were not lost on Mr Pickwick. He settled the spectacles, through which he had attentively regarded such demonstrations of the barrister's feelings as he had permitted himself to exhibit, more firmly on his nose; and said with great energy, and in utter disregard of all Mr Perker's admonitory winkings and frowning –

'My wishing to wait upon you, for such a purpose as this, Sir, appears, I have no doubt, to a gentleman who sees so much of these matters as you must necessarily do, a very extraordinary circumstance.'

The Serjeant tried to look gravely at the fire, but the smile came back again.

'Gentlemen of your profession, Sir,' continued Mr Pickwick, 'see the worst side of human nature – all its disputes, all its ill-will and bad blood, rise up before you. You know from your experience of juries (I mean no disparagement to you, or them) how much depends upon *effect*; and you are apt to attribute to others, a desire to use, for purposes of deception and self-interest, the very instruments which you, in pure honesty and honour of purpose, and with a laudable desire to do your utmost for your client, know the temper and worth of so well, from constantly employing them yourselves. I really believe that to this circumstance may be attributed the vulgar but very general notion of your being, as a body, suspicious, distrustful, and over-cautious. Conscious as I am, sir, of the disadvantage of making such a declaration to you, under such circumstances, I have come here, because I wish you distinctly to understand, as my friend Mr Perker has said, that I am innocent of the falsehood laid to my charge; and although I am very well aware of the inestimable value of your assistance, Sir, I must beg to add, that unless you sincerely believe this, I would rather be deprived of the aid of your talents than have the advantage of them.'

Long before the close of this address, which we are bound to say was of a very prosy character for Mr Pickwick, the Serjeant had relapsed into a state of abstraction.

Now the Serjeant might at once have replied to all this, that the innocence or guilt of a client had nothing to do with him, that his use was merely to secure a client such benefit and advantage as the law entitled him to: that a judge and jury would decided the point of innocence. Boz himself evidently shared this popular delusion, and seems to be speaking by Mr Pickwick's mouth. The sagacious Serjeant, however, took no notice whatever of the appeal, but simply asked 'who was with him' in the case. Mr Phunky was sent for, and asked by his leader 'to take Mr Pickwick away' and 'hear anything he may wish to communicate'. The party was then bowed out.

The truth was Mr Pickwick's attorney was too much of a social character and of the 'old family solicitor' pattern for so critical a case. The counsel he 'instructed' were unsuitable. Serjeant Snubbin was an overworked 'Chamber lawyer', whose whole time and experience was given to furnishing 'opinions' on tangled cases; so pressed was he that he took 'expedition fees' to give certain cases priority: an illegitimate practice that now the Bar Committee would scarcely tolerate. What could such a man know of *nisi prius* trials, of cross-examining or handling witnesses? It is enough to give his portrait, as supplied by the author:

Mr Serjeant Snubbins was a lantern-faced, sallow-complexioned man, of about five-and-forty, or – as the novels say – he might be fifty. He had that *dull-looking boiled eye* which is often to be seen in the heads of people who have applied themselves during many years to a weary and laborious course of study; and which would have been sufficient, without the additional eye-glass which dangled from a broad black riband round his neck, to warn a stranger that he was very near-sighted. His hair was thin and weak, which was partly attributable to his having never devoted much time to its arrangement, and partly to his having worn for five-and-twenty years the forensic wig which hung on a block beside him. The marks of hair powder on his coat collar, and the ill-washed and worse tied white neckerchief round his throat, showed that he had not found leisure since he left the court to make any alteration in his dress; while the slovenly style of the remainder of his costume warranted the inference that his personal appearance would not have been very much improved if he had. Books of practice, heaps of papers, and opened letters, were scattered over the table, without any attempt at order or arrangement; the furniture of the room was old and rickety; the doors of the bookcase were rotting on their hinges; the dust flew out from the carpet in little clouds at every step; the blinds were yellow with age and dirt; the state of everything in the room showed, with a clearness not to be mistaken, that Mr Serjeant Snubbin was far too much occupied with his professional pursuits to take any great heed or regard of his personal comforts.

It was a characteristic feature of the slowness of legal process in those days that though the notice of action was sent on the 28th August 1827, the case was not ripe for trial until 14th February of the next year – nearly six months having elapsed. It is difficult to speculate as to what this long delay was owing. There were only two witnesses whose evidence had to be briefed – Mrs Cluppins and Mrs Saunders – and they were at hand. It is odd, by the way, that they did not think of examining little Tommy Bardell, the only one who actually witnessed the proceeding. True, he was of tender years – about eight or ten – and the son of the plaintiff, but he must have 'known the nature of an oath'.

At last the momentous morning came round. It was the 14th of February, Valentine's Day, 1828 – one not of good omen for the Plaintiff.* The Defendant's party was rather gloomy at breakfast, when Perker, by way of encouraging his client, uttered some *dicta* as to the chances of the Jury having had a good breakfast. 'Discontented or hungry jurymen, my dear Sir, always find for the Plaintiff.'

'Bless my heart,' said Mr Pickwick, looking very blank, 'What do they do that for!'

The party then got into hackney coaches and was driven to the Guildhall, where the case was to be tried at ten o'clock precisely.

How dramatic Boz has made the 'calling of the Jury', which might be thought an uninteresting and prosaic operation enough. It was a special jury, which entailed one guinea per head extra expense on Mr Pickwick. He had, of course, asked for it: but Dodson and Fogg would have been well content with and perhaps even have preferred a common jury. Nowadays, special jurors, though summoned largely, have to be almost coerced into attending. A fine of ten pounds is imposed, but this is almost invariably remitted

---

* So confused is the chronology of *Pickwick*, that it is difficult to fix the exact date of the trial. Boz, writing some ten years after the event, seems to have got a little confused and uncertain as to the exact year of the trial. He first fixed the opening of the story in 1817: but on coming to the compromising incident in Goswell Street, which occurred only a few weeks later, he changed the year to 1827. Then Jingle's anachronism of the French Revolution of July suggested that the new date would not do. So 1830 was next adopted. But this did not end the matter, for in the 'errata' we are directed to change this date back again to 1827. And so it now stands. The trial therefore really took place on 1st April 1828.

on affidavit. The common jurors, moreover, do not show the reluctance to 'serve' of Groffin, the chemist. A guinea is not to be despised. There are, as it were, *professional* common jurors who hang about the courts in the hope of being thus called as 'understudies'. On this occasion what was called a *Tales* was prayed for, and two common jurors were pressed into service: and 'a greengrocer and a chemist were caught directly'.

It is impossible to say too much of the completeness with which the legal scene is put forward. Everything is dealt with. We have perfect sketches of the judge, the ushers, the jury, the counsel on the case, the witnesses, the barristers, the attorneys; we have the speeches, the methods of examination and cross-examination.

There is nothing better or more life-like than the sketch of the court in the chill morning, and before the actors came on the scene – the inimitable description of the idle barristers hanging about 'the Bar of England' which is accurate to this hour.

Few could describe effectively the peculiar appearance of a crowd of barristers assembled in a court of law. They are a type apart, and their odd headgear accentuates all the peculiarities of their faces. No one has, however, succeeded so well as Boz in touching off their peculiarities. This sort of histrionic guise and bearing is assumed with a view to impose on his friends and the public, to suggest an idea that they have much or at least something to do.

'And that,' said Mr Pickwick, pointing to a couple of enclosed seats on his right, 'that's where the jurymen sit, is it not?'

'The identical place, my dear Sir,' replied Perker, tapping the lid of his snuff-box.

Mr Pickwick stood up in a state of great agitation, and took a glance at the court. There were already a pretty large sprinkling of spectators in the gallery, and a numerous muster of gentlemen in wigs in the barristers' seats, who presented, as a body, all that pleasing and extensive variety of nose and whisker for which the Bar of England is so justly celebrated. Such of the gentlemen as had got a brief to carry, carried it in as conspicuous a manner as possible, and occasionally scratched their noses therewith, to impress the fact more strongly on the observation of the spectators.

One of the happiest descriptions is surely that of the binding of law books. A law library is the most repulsive and uninteresting thing in the world. The colour of the leather is unhealthy and disagreeable, and the necessary shading is secured at the expense of grace. Boz characterizes it as 'that under-done pie crust'.

Other gentlemen, who had no briefs to show, carried under their arms goodly octavos, with a red label behind, and that under-done pie-crust-coloured cover, which is technically known as 'law calf'. Others, who had neither briefs nor books, thrust their hands into their pockets, and looked as wise as they conveniently could; while the others, again, moved here and there with great restlessness and earnestness of manner, content to awaken thereby the animation and astonishment of the uninitiated stranger. The whole, to the great wonderment of Mr Pickwick, were divided into little groups, who were chatting and discussing the news of the day in the most unfeeling manner possible – just as if no trial at all were coming on.

A bow from Mr Phunky, as he entered, and took his seat behind the row appropriated to the King's Counsel, attracted Mr Pickwick's attention; and he had scarcely returned it, when Mr Serjeant Snubbin appeared, followed by Mr Mallard, who half hid the Serjeant behind a large crimson bag, which he placed on his table, and after shaking hands with Perker, withdrew. Then there entered two or three more Serjeants, and among them, one with a fat body and a red face, who nodded in a friendly manner to Mr Serjeant Snubbin, and said it was a fine morning.

'Who's that red-faced man, who said it was a fine morning and nodded to our counsel?' whispered Mr Pickwick.

'Mr Serjeant Buzfuz,' replied Perker. 'He's opposed to us; he leads on the other side. That gentleman behind him is Mr Skimpin, his junior.'

Mr Pickwick was just on the point of inquiring, with great abhorrence of the man's cold-blooded villainy, how Mr Serjeant Buzfuz, who was counsel for the opposite party, dared to presume to tell Mr Serjeant Snubbin, who was counsel for him, that it was a fine morning – when he was interrupted by a general rising of the barristers, and a loud cry of 'Silence!' from the officers of the court. Looking round, he found that this was caused by the entrance of the Judge.

On reaching the court, Perker said, 'put Mr Pickwick's friends in the students' box. Mr Pickwick had better sit by me.' This useful provision for the instruction of legal probationers has fallen into desuetude – no place is reserved for the students of nowadays. Lord Campbell describes the custom and recalls an incident that occurred when he was sitting in the students' box, close to the bench.

There were some matters of procedure which have since been changed – such as Mr Skimpin 'calling for' Winkle, and the latter answering. This is now done by an officer of the court. Skimpin also asks Winkle his name, as a first question, though he had been sworn and had given it. And the *mal-entendu* as to 'Daniel Nathaniel' could not then have occurred, as the officer would have obtained the name correctly. Another unusual thing was that Buzfuz, after his long and rather exhausting speech, should have examined the first witness. Nowadays the junior would do this. We may note that at this time it was always 'my Lord' and 'your Lordship', with the full natural sound – we had not yet got to the clipped 'M'lud' and 'your Ludship'. Perhaps this form *was* actually used by the counsel but was not noticed by Boz, or seemed to him the right thing. The King's Counsel were behind and could stoop down to consult their solicitors.

This minute observation and particularity of Boz is further shown in his noting the very places where the attorneys sat, and which he describes. They had the seats next the table:

'You are quite right,' said Buzfuz later on, answering the whisper of Dodson and Fogg, after Sam's awkward revelation. How often have we seen these hasty communications, which are not without their dramatic effect.

Mr Pickwick, unfortunate in his counsel, his solicitor, his jury – one of prejudiced tradesmen – was also to be unlucky in the judge who tried his case. No doubt Perker had comforted him: 'no matter how it goes, however unfair Buzfuz may be, we have a judge to hold the scales fair and keep the jury straight. The Lord Chief Justice of the Common Pleas, the Right Hon. Sir Nicholas Conyngham Tindal, is a man of immense reputation at the Bar. We are most fortunate in having him.' Judge then of the disappointment when on coming to court it was found that Sir Stephen Gaselee was to take the case 'owing to the absence of the Chief Justice, occasioned by indisposition.' (I protest that at times one does not know whether we are following out a course of real events, or tracing the incidents of a fiction, so wonderfully does Boz make his fiction blend with reality.) This was a serious blow. Tindal was an admirable judge. Did not his chroniclers write of him: 'His sagacity, impartiality and plain sense, his industry and clear sightedness made him an admiration of non-professional spectators: while among lawyers he was very highly esteemed for his invariable kindness to all who appeared before him. He retained to the last their respect and affection.' With such a man presiding, Serjeant Buzfuz's eccentric violence and abuse of the defendant would have been restrained ('having the outward appearance of a man and not of a monster'). Mr Skimpin's gross insinuations, to wit, that Winkle was 'telegraphing' to his friend, would have been summarily put down, and all 'bullying' checked; more, he would have calmly kept Counsel's attention to the issue. This perfect impartiality would have made him show to the jury how little evidence there was to support the plaintiff's case. Instead came this unlucky indisposition: and his place was taken by 'my Brother Gaselee': with what results Mr Pickwick was to learn disastrously.

It is curious, however, that the Chief Justice, in spite of his indisposition, should still be associated with the case; for he had tried the momentous case of Norton v. Melbourne, and had heard there letters read, which were parodied in the 'chops and tomato sauce' correspondence, so Boz had him well before him. The case had to be tried at the Guildhall Sessions; so a fair and rational judge would have spoilt all sport. Further, as Boz had seen the fairness and dignity of the Chief Justice he was naturally reluctant to exhibit him unfavourably. The only thing was to make the Chief Justice become suddenly 'indisposed' and have his place taken by a grotesque judge.

The judge who was to try the case, Mr Justice Starcleigh, as is well known, was drawn from Sir Stephen Gaselee, of whose name Stareleigh is a sort of synonym. Serjeant Gaselee was once well known in the prosecutions directed against Radicals and so-called Reformers, but *Pickwick* has given him a greater reputation. The baiting he received from patriotic advocates may have inflamed his temper and made him irritable. He is described by one author, in a most humorous, if personal fashion. He was 'a most particularly short man, and so fat that he seemed all face and waistcoat. He rolled in upon two little turned legs, and having bobbed gravely to the bar who bobbed gravely to him, put his little legs under the table, when all you could see of him was two queer little eyes, one broad, pink face and somewhere about half of a big and very comical-looking wig.' All through he is shown as arrogant and incapable, and also as making some absurd mistakes.

It will be a surprise to most people to learn that this picture is no more than an amusing caricature, and that the judge was really a person of high character. He is described as 'a very painstaking, upright judge, and, in his private capacity, a worthy and benevolent man'. Thus Mr Croker, who, however, supplies a sound reason for his being the subject of such satire. 'With many admirable qualities both of head and heart, he had made himself a legitimate object of ridicule by his explosions on the Bench.' Under such conditions, the Bar, the suitors and the public had neither the wish nor the opportunity to search for extenuating excuses in his private life. They suffered enough from the 'explosions' and that was all that concerned them. He had been fourteen years on the Bench, and, like Stareleigh, belonged to the Common Pleas. He was suffering too from infirmities, particularly from deafness, and appears to have misapprehended statements in the same grotesque fashion that he mistook Winkle's name.

Boz's fashion of burlesque, by the way, is happily shown in his treatment of this topic. Another would have been content with 'Daniel' the simple misapprehension. 'Nathaniel, sir,' says Winkle. 'Daniel – any other name?' 'Nathaniel, sir – my lord, I mean.' '*Nathaniel Daniel – or Daniel Nathaniel?*' 'No, my lord, only Nathaniel, not Daniel at all.'

'What did you tell me it was Daniel for, then, sir?'
'I didn't, my lord.'
'You did, sir. *How could I have got Daniel in my notes, unless you told me so, sir?*'

How admirable is this. The sly satire goes deeper, as judges, under less gross conditions, have often made this illogical appeal to 'my notes'.

Though not gifted with oratorical powers which were likely to gain him employment as a leader, Gaselee's reputation for legal knowledge soon recommended him to a judge's place. He was accordingly selected on 1st July 1824 to fill a vacancy in the Court of Common Pleas. In that court he sat for nearly fourteen years 'with the character of a painstaking judge, and in his private capacity as a worthy and benevolent man'. Thus Mr Foss, F.S.A.

The reader will have noted the judge's severity to poor Groffin, the chemist, who had pleaded the danger of his boy mistaking oxalic acid for Epsom salts. Could it be that the judge's experience as the son of a provincial doctor had shown what class of man was before him? Later, unexpectedly, we learn that the judge was a steady member for fourteen years of the Royal Humane Society, of which institution he was also a vice-president.

But we now come to a most extraordinary thing – the result of the young author's telling and most sarcastic portrait of the irascible little judge. It is curious that Forster, while enumerating various instances of Boz's severe treatment of living persons, as a sort of chastisement for their defects of manner or character, seems not to have thought of this treatment of the judge – and passes it by. Nor did he notice the prompt result that followed on the sketch. The report of the trial appeared in the March number, 1837 – and we are told, the luckless judge retired from the Bench, shortly after the end of Hilary Term, that is in April or the beginning of May. We may assume that the poor gentleman could not endure the jests of his *confrères* or the scarcely concealed tittering of the barristers, all of whom had of course devoured and enjoyed the number. We may say that the learned Serjeant Buzfuz was not likely to be affected in any way by *his* picture; it may indeed have added to his reputation. I confess to some sympathy for the poor old judge who was thus driven from the Bench. Sam Foote was much given to this sort of personal attack, and made the lives of some of his victims wretched. Boz, however, seems to have felt himself called upon to act thus as public executioner on two occasions only. After the fall of the judge in June 1837, he wanted a model for a tyrannical magistrate in *Oliver Twist* – and Mr Laing, the Hatton Garden Magistrate, a harsh and ferocious personage, at once occurred to him. He wrote accordingly to one of his friends that he wished to be *smuggled* into his office some morning to study him. This 'smuggling' of course meant placing him where he would not be observed – as a magistrate knowing his 'sketches' might recognise him. 'I know the man perfectly well,' he added. So he did, for he forgot that he had introduced him already in *Pickwick* as Nupkins – whose talk is exactly alike, in places almost word for word, to that of 'Mr Fang'.

These palliations, Boz, a young fellow of three and twenty or so, did not pause to weigh. He only saw a testy, red-faced old fellow with goggle eyes, and seventy-four years old, and past his work. His infirmities already made him incapable of carrying through the business of the court as the mistake, 'Is it Daniel Nathaniel or Nathaniel Daniel?' shows. It is curious, however, that this weakness of misapprehending names is described of another judge, Arabin – a strange grotesque. Theodore Hook gives an amusing specimen in his Gilbert Gurney.

From the general description in the text, it is evident Stareleigh was the prey of gouty affections – which swelled him into grotesque shape, and he found himself unequal to the office. He died two years after his retirement at No. 13, Montagu Place, Russell Square; so that the judge in Bardell v. Pickwick was living close to Perker the attorney in the same case. Here we seem to mix up the fictional and the living characters, but this is the law of *Pickwick* – the confines between the two worlds being quite confused or broken down. The late commander of our forces in China, Sir A. Gaselee, is of this family. It should be remembered, however, when we think of this judge's forwardness, that judges in those times were dictatorial and carried matters with a high hand. There were often angry conflicts between them, and members of the Bar, and Stareleigh was really not so very tyrannical. He did what so many judges do – took a side from the first, and had decided in his own mind that Mr Pickwick could not possibly have a case. That curious form of address from the Bench is now no longer heard – 'who is with you, *Brother Buzfuz*?' Judges and serjeants were then common members of the Guild – both wore the 'coif'.

When the swearing of the jury is going on, how good, and how natural is the scene with the unfortunate chemist.

'Answer to your names, gentlemen, that you may be sworn,' said the gentleman in black. 'Richard Upwitch.'

'Here,' said the greengrocer.

'Thomas Groffin.'

'Here,' said the chemist.

'Take the book, gentlemen. You shall well and truly try –'

'I beg this court's pardon,' said the chemist, who was a tall, thin, yellow-visaged man, 'but I hope this court will excuse my attendance.'

'On what grounds, Sir?' said Mr Justice Stareleigh.

'I have no assistant, my Lord,' said the chemist.

'I can't help that, Sir,' replied Mr Justice Stareleigh. 'You should hire one.'

'I can't afford it, my Lord,' rejoined the chemist.

'Then you ought to be able to afford it, Sir,' said the judge, reddening; for Mr Justice Stareleigh's temper bordered on the irritable, and brooked not contradiction.

'I know I *ought* to do, if I got on as well as I deserved; but I don't, my Lord,' answered the chemist.

'Swear the gentleman,' said the judge peremptorily.

The officer had got no further than the 'You shall well and truly try,' when he was again interrupted by the chemist.

'Certainly, Sir,' replied the testy little judge.

'Very well, my Lord,' replied the chemist, in a resigned manner. 'Then there'll be murder before this trial's over; that's all. Swear me, if you please, Sir;' and sworn the chemist was, before the judge could find words to utter.

'I merely wanted to observe, my Lord,' said the chemist, taking his seat with great deliberation, 'that I've left nobody but an errand-boy in my shop. He is a very nice boy, my Lord, but he is not acquainted with drugs; and I know that the prevailing impression on his mind is, that Epsom salts means oxalic acid; and syrup of senna, laudanum. That's all, my Lord.' With this, the tall chemist composed himself into a comfortable attitude, and, assuming a pleasant expression of countenance, appeared to have prepared himself for the worst.

One who was born in the same year as Boz, but who was to live for thirty years after him. Henry Russell – composer and singer of 'The Ivy Green' – was, when a youth, apprenticed to a chemist, and when about ten years old, that is five years before Bardell v. Pickwick, was left in charge of the shop. He discovered just in time that he had served a customer who had asked for Epsom salts with poison sufficient to kill fifty people. On this he gave up the profession. I have little doubt that he told this story to his friend a dozen years later, and that it was on Boz's mind when he wrote. Epsom salts was the drug mentioned in both instances.

It must be said that even in our day a defendant for breach, with Mr Pickwick's story and surroundings, would have had small chance with a city jury. They saw before them a benevolent-looking Lothario, of a Quaker-like air, while all the witnesses against him were his three most intimate friends and his own man.

We have, of course, testy judges now, who may be 'short' in manner, but I think it can be affirmed that no judge of our day could behave to counsel or witnesses as Mr Justice Stareleigh did. It is, in fact, not the tone for a judge to impart a sort of light gaiety to the business he is transacting. All asperity and tyrannous rudeness is held to be out of place. Hectoring and bullying of witnesses will not be tolerated. The last exhibition was perhaps that of the late Dr Kenealy in the Tichborne case.

All the swearing of the jurymen before the court, with the intervention of the judge, has been got rid of. The Master of the Court, or Chief Clerk, has a number of interviews – at his public desk – with important individuals, bringing him signed papers. These are excuses of some sort – medical certificates, etc. – with a view to be 'let off' serving. Some – most, perhaps – are accepted, some refused. A man of wealth and importance can have little difficulty. Of course this would be denied by the jurists: but, somehow, the great guns contrive not to attend. At ten o'clock this officer proceeds to swear the jury, which is happily accomplished by the time the judge enters.

Mr Pickwick, considering the critical nature of his case, was certainly unfortunate in his solicitor, as well as in the counsel selected by his solicitors. The other side were particularly favoured in this matter. They had a pushful bustling 'wide-awake' firm of solicitors, who let not a point escape. Serjeant Buzfuz was exactly the sort of advocate for the case – masterful, unscrupulous, eloquent, and with a singularly ingenious faculty for putting everything on his client's side in the best light, and his adversary's in the worst. He could 'tear a witness to pieces', and turn him inside out. His junior, Skimpin, was glib, ready-armed at all points, and singularly adroit in 'making a hare' of any witness who fell into his hands, *teste* Winkle. He had all the professional devices for dealing with a witness's answers, and twisting them to his purpose, at his fingers' ends. He was the Wontner or Ballantyne of his day. Mr Pickwick's 'bar' was quite outmatched. They were rather a feeble lot, too respectable altogether, and really not familiar with this line of business. Even the judge was against them from the very start, so Mr Pickwick had very poor chances indeed. All this was due to that old-fashioned and rather incapable 'Family Solicitor' Perker.

Serjeant Buzfuz is known the world all over, at least wherever English is known. I myself was once startled in a fashionable West End church to hear a preacher, when emphasizing the value and necessity of prayer, and the certainty with which it is responded to, use this illustration: 'As Serjeant Buzfuz said to Sam Weller, "*There is little to do and plenty to get.*"' Needless to say, an amused smile, if not a titter, passed round the congregation. But it is the barrister who most appreciates the learned Serjeant. For the topics he argued and his fashion of arguing them, bating a not excessive exaggeration, comes home to them all. Nay, they must have a secret admiration, and fondly think how excellently well such and such topics are put, and how they must have told with a jury.

Buzfuz, it is now well known, was drawn from a leading serjeant of his day, Serjeant Bompas, K.C. Not so long since I was sitting by Bompas's son, the present Judge Bompas, at dinner, and a most agreeable causeur he was. Not only did Boz sketch the style and fashion of the serjeant, but it is clear that Phiz drew the figure and features.

'I am the youngest son of Serjeant Bompas,' Judge Bompas writes to me, 'and have never heard I doubted that the name Buzfuz was taken from my father, who was at that time considered a most successful advocate. I think he may have been chosen for the successful advocate because he was so successful: but I have never been able to ascertain that there was any other special resemblance. I do not remember my father myself: he died when I was eight years old. But I am told I am like him in face. He was tall (five feet ten inches) and a large man, very popular, and very excitable in his cases, so that I am told that counsel against him used to urge him, out of friendship, not to get so agitated. A connection of mine who knew him well, went over to hear Charles Dickens read the trial scene, to see if he at all imitated him in voice or manner, but told me that he did not do so at all. I think, therefore, that having chosen his name, as a writer might now that of Sir Charles Russell, he then drew a general type of barrister, as he thought it might be satirised. My father, like myself, was on the Western Circuit and leader of it at the time of his death.

'I had a curious episode happen to me once. A client wrote to apply to the court to excuse a juror on the ground that he was a chemist and had no assistant who understood the drugs. It was not till I made the application and the court begun to laugh that I remembered the Pickwick trial. I believe the application was quite bona fide, and not at all an imitation of it.' An interesting communication from one who might be styled 'Buzfuz's son'; and, as Judge Bompas alludes to his own likeness to his sire, I may add the likeness to the portrait in the court scene, is very striking indeed. There is the same fullness of face, the large features. Buzfuz was certainly a counsel of power and ability, and I think lawyers will admit he managed Mrs Bardell's case with much adroitness. His speech, besides being a sort of satirical abstract of the unamiable thundering boisterousness addressed to juries in such cases, is one of much ability. He makes the most of every topic that he thought likely to 'tell' on a city jury. We laugh heartily at his would-be solemn and pathetic passages, but these are little exaggerated. Buzfuz's statement is meant to show how counsel, quite legitimately, can bring quite innocent acts to the support of their case by marshalling them in suspicious order, and suggesting that they had a connection with the charge made. Many a client thus becomes as bewildered as Mr Pickwick was, on seeing his harmless proceedings assuming quite a guilty complexion.

Serjeant Buzfuz-Bompas died at the age of fifty-three, at his house in Park Road, Regents Park, on 29th February 1844. He was then, comparatively, a young man, and must have had ability to have attained his position so early. He was called to the Bar in 1815, and began as Serjeant in 1827, in Trinity Term, only a year or so before the famous case was tried.

So dramatic is the whole 'trial' in its action and characters that it is almost fit for the stage as it stands. There have been a great number of versions, one by the author's son, Charles 'the younger', one by Mr Holingshead, and so on. It is a favourite piece for charitable benefits, and a number of well-known performers often volunteer to figure as 'Gentlemen of the Jury'. Buzfuz has been often played by Mr Toole, but his too farcical methods scarcely enhanced the part. The easiness of comedy is essential. That sound player Mr James Fernandez is the best Buzfuz that I have seen.

There is a French translation of *Pickwick*, in which the general spirit of the 'trial' is happily conveyed. Thus Mr Phunky's name is given as 'M. Finge', which the little judge mistakes for 'M. Singe'. Buzfuz's speech too is excellent, especially his denouncing the defendant's coming with his chops '*et son ignoble bassinoire*', i.e., warming-pan.

Buzfuz's great speech is one of the happiest parodies in the language. Never was the forensic jargon and treatment so humorously set forth – and this because of the perfect *sincerity* and earnestness with which it was done. There is none of the far-fetched, impossible exaggeration – the form of burlesque which Theodore Hook or Albert Smith might have attempted. It is, in fact, a real speech, which might have been delivered to a dull-headed audience without much impairing credibility. Apart from this it is a most effective harangue and most plausible statement of the plaintiff's case.

A little professional touch, which is highly significant as part of the pantomime, and which Boz made very effective at the reading, was the Serjeant's dramatic preparation for his speech. 'Having whispered to Dodson and conferred briefly with Fogg, *he pulled his gown over his shoulders, settled his wig*, and addressed the Jury.' Who has not seen this bit of business?

Again, juries may have noted that the junior as he rises to speak, mumbles something that is quite inaudible, and which nobody attends to. This is known as 'opening the pleadings'.

> The ushers again called silence, and Mr Skimpin proceeded to 'open the case'; and the case appeared to have very little inside it when he had opened it, for he kept such particulars as he knew, completely to himself, and sat down, after a lapse of three minutes, leaving the jury in precisely the same advanced stage of wisdom as they were in before.
>
> Serjeant Buzfuz then rose with all the majesty and dignity which the grave nature of the proceeding demanded and having whispered to Dodson, and conferred

briefly with Fogg, pulled his gown over his shoulders, settled his wig, and addressed the jury.

A most delightful legal platitude, as one might call it, is to be found in the opening of the learned Serjeant's speech. It is a familiar, transparent thing, often used to impose on the Jury. As Boz says of another topic, 'Counsel often begins in this way because it makes the jury think what sharp fellows they must be.'

'You have heard from my learned friend, gentlemen,' continued the Serjeant, well knowing that from the learned friend alluded to they had heard just nothing at all, 'you have heard from my learned friend, that this is an action for Breach of Promise of Marriage, in which the damages are laid at £1,500. But you have *not heard from my learned friend, inasmuch as it did not lie within my learned friend's province to tell you*, what are the facts and circumstances of the case.'

This rich bit of circumlocution is simple nonsense, in rotund phrase, and meant to suggest the imposing majesty of legal process. The jury knew perfectly beforehand what they were going to try: but were to be impressed by the magnifying agency of legal processes, and would be awestricken accordingly. The passage, 'inasmuch as it did not lie within my learned friend's province to tell you', is a delightful bit of cant. In short, the jury was thus admitted to the secret legal arena, and into community with the learned friends themselves, and were persuaded that they were very sharp fellows indeed. What pleasant satire is here, on the mellifluous 'openings' of counsel, the putting a romantic gloss on the most prosaic incidents.

A sucking barrister might well study this speech of Buzfuz as a guide to the conducting of a case, and above all of rather a 'shaky' one. Not less excellent is his smooth and plausible account of Mrs Bardell's setting up in lodging letting. He really makes it 'interesting'. One thinks of some fluttering, helpless young widow, setting out in the battle of life.

He describes the poor innocent lady putting a bill in her window:

...and let me entreat the attention of the Jury to the wording of this document – 'Apartments furnished for a single gentleman!' Mrs Bardell's opinions of the opposite sex, gentlemen, were derived from a long contemplation of inestimable qualities of her lost husband. She had no fear – she had no distrust – she had no suspicion – all was confidence and reliance. 'Mr Bardell,' said the widow: 'Mr Bardell was a man of honour – Mr Bardell was a man of his word – Mr Bardell was no deceiver – Mr Bardell was once a single gentleman himself; to single gentlemen I look for protection, for assistance, for comfort, and for consolation – in single gentlemen I shall perpetually see something to remind me of what Mr Bardell was when he first won my young and untried affections; to a single gentleman, then, shall my lodgings be let.' Actuated by this beautiful and touching impulse (among the best impulses of our imperfect nature, gentlemen), the lonely and desolate widow dried her tears, furnished her first floor, caught her innocent boy to her maternal bosom, and put the bill up in her parlour window. Did it remain there long? No. The serpent was on the watch, the train was laid, the mine was preparing, the sapper and miner was at work. Before the bill had been in the parlour window three days – three days, gentlemen – a being, erect upon two legs, and bearing all the outward semblance of a man, and not of a monster, knocked at the door of Mrs Bardell's house. He inquired within.

Those who attended the reading will recall the admirable briskness, and more admirable spirit with which Boz delivered the passage 'by the evidence of the unimpeachable female whom I shall place in that' – here he brought down his palm with a mighty slap on the desk, and added, after a moment's pause, '*Box* before you.' It was that *preceding* of the stroke that told. So real was it, one fancied oneself listening to some obstreperous counsel. In all true acting – notable on the French boards – the gesture should a little precede the utterance. So the Serjeant knew something of art.

When Mr Pickwick gave an indignant start on hearing himself described as a heartless villain how cleverly does the capable Buzfuz turn the incident to profit.

'I say systematic villainy, gentlemen,' said Serjeant Buzfuz, looking through Mr Pickwick, and talking *at* him; 'and when I say systematic villainy, let me tell the defendant, Pickwick, if he be in court, as I am informed he is, that it would have been more decent in him, more becoming, in better judgment, and in better taste, if he had stopped away. Let me tell him, gentlemen, that any gestures of dissent or disapprobation in which he may indulge in this court will not go down with you; that you will know how to value and how to appreciate them; and let me tell him further, as my Lord will tell you, gentlemen, that a counsel, in the discharge of his duty to his client, is neither to be intimidated nor bullied, nor put down; and that any attempt to do either the one or the other, or the first, or the last, will recoil on the head of the attempter, be he plaintiff or be he defendant, be his name Pickwick, or Noakes, or Stoakes, or Stiles, or Brown, or Thompson.'

This little divergence from the subject in hand, had of course the intended effect of turning all eyes to Mr Pickwick.

We relish, too, another 'common form'. When the Serjeant found that his jest as to 'greasing the wheels of Mr Pickwick's slow-coach' had somewhat misfired – a thing that often unaccountably happens, in the case of the 'twelve intelligent men' – the Serjeant knew how to adroitly recover himself.

He paused in this place, to see whether the jury smiled at his joke; but as nobody took it but the greengrocer, whose sensitiveness on the subject was very probably occasioned by his having subjected a chaise-cart to the process in question on that identical morning, the learned Serjeant considered it advisable to undergo a slight relapse into the dismals before he concluded.

'But enough of this, gentlemen,' said Mr Serjeant Buzfuz, 'it is difficult to smile with an aching heart; it is ill jesting when our deepest sympathies are awakened. My client's hopes and prospects are ruined, and it is no figure of speech to say that her occupation is gone indeed. The bill is down – but there is no tenant. Eligible single gentlemen pass and repass – but there is no invitation for to inquire within or without. All is gloom and silence in the house; even the voice of the child is hushed; his infant sports are disregarded when his mother weeps; his "alley tors" and his "commoneys" are alike neglected; he forgets the long familiar cry of "knuckle down", and at tip-cheese, or odd and even, his hand is out. But Pickwick, gentlemen, Pickwick, the ruthless destroyer of this domestic oasis in the desert of Goswell Street – Pickwick who has choked up the well, and thrown ashes on the sward – Pickwick, who comes before you today with his heartless tomato sauce and warming-pans – Pickwick still rears his head with un-blushing effrontery, and gazes without a sigh on the ruin he has made. Damages, gentlemen – heavy damages is the only punishment with which you can visit him.'

'I shall prove to you, gentlemen, that *about a year ago, Pickwick suddenly began to absent himself from home*, during long intervals, [on 'Pickwick Tours'] *as if with the intention of gradually breaking off from my client*; but I shall show you also that his resolution was not at that time sufficiently strong, or that his better feelings conquered, *if better feelings he has*, or that the charms and accomplishments of my client prevailed against his unmanly intentions.' We may note the reserve which suggested a struggle going on in Mr Pickwick. And how persuasive is Buzfuz's *exegesis*.

These letters bespeak the character of the man. They are not open, fervent, eloquent epistles, breathing nothing but the language of affectionate attachment. They are *covert*, *sly*, underhanded communications, but, fortunately, far more conclusive than if couched in the most glowing language. *Letters that must be viewed with a cautious and suspicious eye: letters that were evidently intended at the time, by Pickwick, to mislead and delude any third parties into whose hands they might fall.*

The gravity and persuasiveness of all this is really *impayable*.

Let me read the first: 'Garraways, twelve o'clock. Dear Mrs B. – Chops and tomato sauce. Yours, Pickwick.' Gentlemen, what does this mean? Chops and tomato sauce. Yours, Pickwick! Chops! Gracious heavens! – and tomato sauce! Gentlemen, is the happiness of a sensitive and confiding female *to be trifled* away, by such shallow artifices as these? *The next has no date whatever, which is in itself suspicious.*

'Dear Mrs B., I shall not be at home till to-morrow. Slow coach.' And then follows this very remarkable expression, 'Don't trouble yourself about the warming-pan.'

There is a little bit of serious history connected with these letters which I was the first I think to discover. They were intended to satirise the trivial scraps brought forward in Mrs Norton's matrimonial case – Norton v. Lord Melbourne. My late friend, 'Charles Dickens the younger', as he used to call himself, in his notes on *Pickwick*, puts aside this theory altogether as a mere unfounded fancy; but it will be seen there cannot be a doubt in the matter. Sir W. Follett laid just as much stress on these scraps as Serjeant Buzfuz did on his: he even used the phrase, 'it seems there may be latent love like latent heat, in these productions'. We have also, 'Yours Melbourne', like 'Yours Pickwick', the latter signing as though he were a Peer. 'There is another of these notes,' went on Sir William, 'How are you?' 'Again there is no beginning you see.' 'The next has no date, which is in itself suspicious,' Buzfuz would have added. Another ran – 'I will call about half past four, Yours.' '*These* are the only notes that have been found,' added the counsel, with due gravity, '*they seem to import much more than mere words convey.*' After this can there be a doubt?'

This case was tried in June, 1836, and, it must be borne in mind, caused a prodigious sensation all over the kingdom. The Pickwick part, containing the description, appeared about December, six months afterwards. Only old people may recall Norton v. Melbourne, the fair Caroline's wrongs have long been forgotten; but it is curious that the memory of it should have been kept alive in some sort by this farcical parody. Equally curious is it that the public should always have insisted that she was the heroine of yet another story, George

Meredith's *Diana*, though the author has disclaimed it over and over again.

The Serjeant's dealing with the warming-pan topic is a truly admirable satiric touch, and not one bit far-fetched or exaggerated. Anyone familiar with suspicious actions has again and again heard comments as plausible and as forced. 'Don't trouble yourself about the warming-pan! The warming-pan! Why, gentlemen, who *does* trouble himself about a warming-pan?' A delicious *non sequitur*, sheer nonsense, and yet with an air of conviction that is irresistible. 'When was the peace of mind of man or woman broken or disturbed by a warming-pan which is in itself a harmless, a useful *and I will add, gentlemen*, a comforting article of domestic furniture?' He then goes on ingeniously to suggest that it may be 'a cover for hidden fire, a mere substitute for some endearing word or promise, *agreeably to a preconcerted system* of correspondence, artfully contrived by Pickwick *with a view* to his contemplated desertion and which I am not in a position to explain?' Admirable indeed! One could imagine a city jury in their wisdom thinking that there must be *something* in this warming pan!

Not less amusing and plausible is his dealing with the famous topic of the 'chops and tomato sauce', not 'tomata' as Boz has it. I suppose there is no popular allusion better understood than this. The very man in the street knows all about it and what it means. Absurd as it may seem, it is hardly an exaggeration. Counsel every day give weight to points just as trivial and expound them elaborately to the jury. The Serjeant's burst of horror is admirable, 'Gentlemen, *what does this mean*? "Chops and tomata sauce! Yours Pickwick!" Chops! Gracious Heavens! What does this mean? Is the happiness of a sensitive and confiding female to be trifled away, *by such shallow artifices as these*?'

I recall that admirable judge and pleasant man, the late Lord FitzGerald, who was fond of talking of this trial, saying to me that Buzfuz lost a good point here, as he might have dwelt on the mystic meaning of tomato which is the 'love apple', that here was the 'secret correspondence', the real 'cover for hidden fire'.

He concluded by demanding exemplary damages as 'the recompense you can award my client. And for these damages she now appeals to an enlightened, a high-minded, a right feeling, a conscientious, a dispassionate, a sympathising, a contemplative jury of her civilized countrymen!'

It was really of a very flimsy kind but 'bolstered up' and carried through by the bluster of the Serjeant and the smartness of his junior. It rested first on a dialogue between Mr Pickwick and his landlady which was overheard, in fact by several persons; second, on a striking situation witnessed by his three friends who entered unexpectedly and surprised him with Mrs Bardell in his arms; third, on some documentary evidence, and lastly, on a damaging incident disclosed by Winkle.

The first witness 'put in the box' was Mrs Martha Cluppins – an intimate friend of the plaintiffs.

We know that she was sister to Mrs Raddle, who lived far away in Southwark, and was the landlady of Mr Sawyer. She might have been cross-examined with effect as to her story that she had been 'out buying kidney pertaties' etc. Why buy these articles in Goswell Street and come all the way from Southwark? What was she doing there at all? This question could have been answered only in one way – which was that the genial author fancied at the moment she was living near Mrs Bardell.

Beside this, there was another point which Snubbin, in cross-examination, ought to have driven home. Mrs Cluppins was of an inferior type, of the common washerwoman or 'charing' sort; her language was of Mrs Gamp's kind; 'which her name was' so and so. Yet, this creature, in another room, or on the stairs, the door being 'on the jar', can repeat with her limited appreciation, those dubious and imperfect utterances of Mr Pickwick! How could she remember them all? Or could she understand them? Impossible! She, however, may have caught up something.

Winkle, too, said he heard something as he came up the stairs: 'Compose yourself my dear creatures, for consider if any one were to come,' etc. But what could be the value of evidence heard in this way? Would a jury believe it? Not only, as Sam said, is 'wision limited', but hearing also.

In short, the delicate subtleties of the conversation between Mr Pickwick and Mrs Bardell would be wholly lost in her hands. Persons of her class know nothing of suggestion or double meanings or reserved intention, everything for them must be in black and white. How unlikely, therefore, that through the panels of a door or through the half opened door, ('she said on the jar') could she catch the phrases and their meanings, and, above all, retain them in her memory? No doubt, as the counsel put it bluntly, she listened, and with all her ears.

However this may be, here is what Mrs Cluppins deposed to:

'Mrs Cluppins,' said Serjeant Buzfuz, 'pray compose yourself, ma'am.' Of course, directly Mrs Cluppins was desired to compose herself, she sobbed with increased violence, and gave divers alarming manifestations of an approaching fainting fit, or, as she afterwards said, of her feelings being too many for her.

'Do you recollect, Mrs Cluppins,' said Serjeant Buzfuz, after a few unimportant questions – 'do you recollect being in Mrs Bardell's back one pair of stairs, on one particular morning in July last, when she was dusting Pickwick's apartment?'

'Yes, my Lord and jury, I do,' replied Mrs Cluppins.

'Mr Pickwick's sitting-room was the first floor front, I believe?'

'Yes, it were, Sir,' replied Mrs Cluppins.

'What were you doing in the back room, ma'am?' inquired the little judge.

'My Lord and jury,' said Mrs Cluppins, with interesting agitation, 'I will not deceive you.'

'You had better not, ma'am,' said the little judge.

'I was there,' resumed Mrs Cluppins, 'unbeknown to Mrs Bardell; I had been out with a little basket, gentlemen, to buy three pound of red kidney pertaties, which was three pound tuppence ha'penny, when I see Mrs Bardell's street door on the jar.'

'On the what?' exclaimed the little judge.

'Partly open, my Lord,' said Serjeant Snubbin.

'She *said* on the jar,' said the little judge, with a cunning look.

'It's all the same, my Lord,' said Serjeant Snubbin. The little judge looked doubtful, and said he'd make a note of it. Mrs Cluppins then resumed

'I walked in, gentlemen, just to say good mornin', and went, in a permiscuous manner, up-stairs, and into the back room. Gentlemen, there was the sound of voices in the front room, and –'

'And you listened, I believe, Mrs Cluppins?' said Serjeant Buzfuz.

'Beggin' your pardon, Sir,' replied Mrs Cluppins, in a majestic manner, 'I would scorn the haction. The voices was very loud, Sir, and forced themselves upon my ear.'

'Well, Mrs Cluppins, you were not listening, but you heard the voices. Was one of those voices Mr Pickwick's?'

'Yes, it were, Sir.'

And Mrs Cluppins, after distinctly stating that Mr Pickwick addressed himself to Mrs Bardell, repeated by slow degrees, and by dint of many questions, the conversation with which our readers are already acquainted.

Now we have to turn back to one of the earlier passages in the story for the conversation between the pair, 'with which the reader is already acquainted'. Thus we shall know what Mrs Cluppins might have heard.

Mr Pickwick paced the room to and fro with hurried steps, popped his head out of the window at intervals of about three minutes each, constantly referred to his watch, and exhibited many other manifestations of impatience very unusual with him. It was evident that something of great importance was in contemplation, but what that something was, not even Mrs Bardell had been enabled to discover.

'Mrs Bardell,' said Mr Pickwick, at last, as that amiable female approached the termination of a prolonged dusting of the apartment.

'Sir,' said Mrs Bardell.

'Your little boy is a very long time gone.'

'Why it's a good long way to the Borough, sir,' remonstrated Mrs Bardell.

'Ah,' said Mr Pickwick, 'very true; so it is.'

Mr Pickwick relapsed into silence, and Mrs Bardell resumed her dusting.

'Mrs Bardell,' said Mr Pickwick, at the expiration of a few minutes.

'Sir,' said Mrs Bardell again.

'Do you think it a much greater expense to keep two people, than to keep one?'

'La, Mr Pickwick,' said Mrs Bardell, colouring up to the very border of her cap, as she fancied she observed a species of matrimonial twinkle in the eyes of her lodger; 'La, Mr Pickwick, what a question!'

'Well, but *do* you?' inquired Mr Pickwick.

'That depends,' said Mrs Bardell, approaching the duster very near to Mr Pickwick's elbow which was planted on the table; 'that depends a good deal upon the person, you know, Mr Pickwick; and whether it's a saving and careful person, sir.'

'That's very true,' said Mr Pickwick, 'but the person I have in my eye (here he looked very hard at Mrs Bardell) I think possesses these qualities; and has, moreover, a considerable knowledge of the world, and a great deal of sharpness, Mrs Bardell, which may be of material use to me.'

'La, Mr Pickwick,' said Mrs Bardell, the crimson rising to her cap-border again.

'I do,' said Mr Pickwick, growing energetic, as was his wont in speaking of a subject which interested him, 'I do, indeed; and to tell you the truth, Mrs Bardell, I have made up my mind.'

'Dear me, sir,' exclaimed Mrs Bardell.

'You'll think it very strange now,' said the amiable Mr Pickwick, with a good-humoured glance at his companion, 'that I never consulted you about this matter, and never even mentioned it, till I sent your little boy out this morning, eh?'

Mrs Bardell could only reply by a look. She had long worshipped Mr Pickwick at a distance, but here she was, all at once, raised to a pinnacle to which her wildest and most extravagant hopes had never dared to aspire. Mr Pickwick was going to propose – a deliberate plan, too – sent her little boy to the Borough, to get him out of the way – how thoughtful – how considerate!

'Well,' said Mr Pickwick, 'what do you think?'

'Oh, Mr Pickwick,' said Mrs Bardell, trembling with agitation, 'you're very kind, sir.'

'It'll save you a good deal of trouble, won't it?' said Mr Pickwick.

'Oh, I never thought anything of the trouble, sir,' replied Mrs Bardell; 'and, of course, I should take more trouble to please you then, than ever; but it is so kind of you, Mr Pickwick, to have so much consideration for my loneliness.'

'Ah, to be sure,' said Mr Pickwick; 'I never thought of that. When I am in town, you'll always have somebody to sit with you. To be sure, so you will.'

'I am sure I ought to be a very happy woman,' said Mrs Bardell.

'And your little boy –' said Mr Pickwick.

'Bless his heart!' interposed Mrs Bardell, with a maternal sob.

'He, too, will have a companion,' resumed Mr Pickwick, 'a lively one, who'll teach him, I'll be bound, more tricks in a week than he would ever learn in a year.' And Mr Pickwick smiled placidly.

'Oh, you dear –' said Mrs Bardell.

Mr Pickwick started.

'Oh, you kind, good, playful dear,' said Mrs Bardell; and without more ado, she rose from her chair, and flung her arms round Mr Pickwick's neck, with a cataract of tears and a chorus of sobs.

'Bless my soul,' cried the astonished Mr Pickwick; 'Mrs Bardell, my good woman – dear me, what a situation – pray – consider, Mrs Bardell, if anybody should come –'

'Oh, let them come,' exclaimed Mrs Bardell frantically; 'I'll never leave you, dear, kind, good soul.' And, with these words, Mrs Bardell clung the tighter.

Every utterance of the little judge is in character from his first directions 'go on'. His suspicious question, 'what were you doing in the back room, ma'am?' – and on Serjeant Buzfuz's sudden pause for breath, when 'the *silence* awoke Mr Justice Stareleigh, who immediately wrote down something, with a pen without any ink in it, and looked unusually profound, to impress his jury with the belief that he always thought most deeply with his eyes shut'. Also when at the 'on the jar' incident – he 'looked doubtful, but said he'd make a note of it'. So when Sam made one of his free and easy speeches, the judge looked sternly at Sam for fully two minutes, but Sam's features were so perfectly calm that he said nothing. When Sam, too, made his witty *riposte* to Buzfuz as to his 'wision being limited', we are told that there was a great laugh – that even 'the little Judge smiled': a good touch, for he enjoyed, like other judges, seeing his learned brother get a fall – 'tis human nature.

It must be said the impression of a listener, who had heard all this, could have been anything but favourable to Mr Pickwick. No doubt there was his paternally benevolent character to correct it: but even this might go against him as it would suggest a sort of hypocrisy. Even the firmest friends, in their surprise, do not pause to debate or reason; they are astonished and wonder exceedingly.

Skimpin may have been intended for Wilkin, a later Serjeant and well-known in the fifties, and whose style and manner is reproduced. We could not ask a better junior in a 'touch and go' case. He was as ready to take advantage of any opening as was the late Lord Bowen, when he was junior in the Tichborne case.

On entering the box, Mr Winkle 'bowed to the Judge' with considerable deference, a politeness quite thrown away. 'Don't look at me, sir,' said the judge sharply, 'look at the Jury.' This was ungracious, but judges generally don't relish any advances from witnesses or others.

When poor Winkle was accused by the judge of giving his name as Daniel, he was told that 'he had better be careful', on which the ready Skimpin: 'Now Mr Winkle attend to me if you please: and let me recommend for your own sake to bear in mind his lordship's injunction to be careful.' Thus by the agency of the judge and counsel, witness was discredited at starting and of course flurried.

'I believe you are a particular friend of Mr Pickwick, the defendant, are you not?'

'I have known Mr Pickwick now, as well as I recollect at this moment, nearly –'

'Pray, Mr Winkle, do not evade the question. Are you, or are you not, a particular friend of the defendant's?'

'I was just about to say, that –'

'Will you, or will you not, answer my question, Sir?'

'If you don't answer you'll be committed, Sir,' interposed the little judge.

'Come, Sir,' said Mr Skimpin, *'yes or no, if you please.'*

'Yes, I am,' replied Mr Winkle.

'*Yes, you are. And why couldn't you say that at once, Sir?*'

I think there is no more happy touch of legal satire in the books than that about 'What the soldier said.' It is perfect. So complete, that it is always understood by unprofessional readers. The lawyer feels at once that it is as true as it is happy.

'Little to do, and plenty to get, I suppose?' said Serjeant Buzfuz, with jocularity.

'Oh, quite enough to get, Sir, as the soldier said ven they ordered him three hundred and fifty lashes,' replied Sam.

'*You must not tell us what the soldier or any other man said, Sir; it's not evidence,*' interposed the Judge.

Who will forget the roar that always greeted this sally when Boz read it, or the low and slow solemnity which he imparted to the Judge's dictum. As an illustration it is simply admirable.

Boz himself would have been pleased to find himself quoted in two impressive legal tomes of some 1,800 pages. The great and laborious John Pitt Taylor could not have been wholly a legal dry-as-dust: for the man who could have gravely entered Bardell v. Pickwick in his notes and have quoted a passage must have had a share of humour.

Most people know that it is a strict principle that 'hearsay evidence' of an utterance will not be accepted in lieu of that of the person to whom the remark was made. Neither can we think it out of probability that such an objection may have been made by some over-punctilious judge wishing to restrain Sam's exuberance. A Scotch judge once quoted in court a passage from *The Antiquary* in which he said the true view of an intricate point was given; but then Scott was a lawyer.

It is requisite, says Mr John Pitt Taylor (p. 500), speaking of 'hearsay' evidence, that whatever facts a witness speaks, he should be confined to those lying within his own knowledge. For every witness should give his testimony on oath, and should be subject to cross-examination. But testimony from the relation of third persons cannot be subject to these tests. This rule of exclusion has been recognised as a fundamental principle of the law of evidence ever since the time of Charles II. To this he adds a note, with all due gravity: 'The rules excluding heresay evidence, or rather the mode in which that rule is frequently misunderstood in Courts of Justice, is amusingly caricatured by Mr Dickens *in his report* of the case of Bardell v. Pickwick, p. 367.'

Bardell v. Pickwick! He thus puts it with the many thousands or tens of thousand cases quoted, and he has even found a place for it in his index of cases. He then goes on to quote the passage, just as he would quote from Barnwall and Adolphus.

How sagacious – full of legal point – is Boz's comment on Winkle's incoherent evidence. Phunky asked him whether he had any reason to suppose that Pickwick was about to be married. '"Oh no; certainly not," replied Mr Winkle with so much eagerness, that Mr Phunky ought to have got him out of the box with all possible dispatch. Lawyers hold out that there are two kinds of particularly bad witnesses – a reluctant witness, and a too-willing witness,' and most true it is. Both commit themselves in each case, but in different ways. The matter of the former, and the manner of the latter do the mischief. The ideal witness affects indifference, and is as impartial as the record of a phonograph. It is wonderful where Boz learned all this. No doubt from his friend Talfourd, K.C., who carefully revised 'The Trial'.

Skimpin's interpretation of Mr Pickwick's consolatory phrase, which he evidently devised on the spur of the moment, shows him to be a very ready, smart fellow.

'Now, Mr Winkle, I have only one more question to ask you, and I beg you to bear in mind his Lordship's caution. Will you undertake to swear that Pickwick, the defendant, did not say on the occasion in question –"My dear Mrs Bardell, you're a good creature; compose yourself to this situation, for to this situation you must come," or words to that effect?'

'I–I didn't understand him so, certainly,' said Mr Winkle, astounded on this ingenious dove-tailing of the few words he had heard. 'I was on the staircase, and couldn't hear distinctly; the impression on my mind is –'

'The gentlemen of the jury want none of the impressions on your mind, Mr Winkle, which I fear would be of little service to honest, straightforward men,' interposed Mr Skimpin. 'You were on the staircase, and didn't distinctly hear; but you will not swear that Pickwick *did not make use* of the expressions I have quoted? Do I understand that?'

'No, I will not,' replied Mr Winkle; and down sat Mr Skimpin with a triumphant countenance.

This 'Will you swear he did *not*' etc. is a device familiar to cross-examiners, and is used when the witness cannot be got to accept the words or admit that they were used. It of course means little or nothing: but the effect on the jury is that they come to fancy the words *may* have been used, and that the witness is not very clear as to his recollection.

How well described, too, and satirized, is yet another 'common form' of the cross-examiner, to wit the 'How often,

Sir' question. Winkle, when asked as to his knowledge of Mrs Bardell, replied that 'he did not know her, but that he had seen her.' (I recall making this very answer to Boz when we were both driving through Sackville Street, Dublin. He had asked 'Did I know so-and-so?' when I promptly replied, 'I don't know him, but I have seen him.' This rather arrided him, as Elia would say.)

Skimpin went on: 'Oh, you don't know her, but you have seen her.

'Now have the goodness to tell the gentlemen of the jury what you mean by *that*, Mr Winkle.'

'I mean that I am not intimate with her, but that I have seen her when I went to call on Mr Pickwick, in Goswell Street.'

'How often have you seen her, Sir?'

'How often?'

'*Yes, Mr Winkle, how often?* I'll repeat the question for you a dozen times, if you require it, Sir.' And the learned gentleman, with a firm and steady frown, placed his hands on his hips, and smiled suspiciously to the jury.

On this question there arose the edifying brow-beating, customary on such points. First of all, Mr Winkle said it was quite impossible for him to say how many times he had seen Mrs Bardell. Then he was asked if he had seen her twenty times, to which he replied, 'Certainly, more than that.' And then he was asked whether he hadn't seen her a hundred times – whether he couldn't swear that he had seen her more than fifty times – whether he didn't know that he had seen her at least seventy-five times, and so forth; the satis-factory conclusion which was arrived at, at last, being – that he had better take care of himself, and mind what he was about. The witness having been, by these means, reduced to the requisite ebb of nervous perplexity, the examination was concluded.

How excellent is this. Who has not heard the process repeated over and over again from the young fledgling counsel to the old 'hardbitten' and experienced K.C.?

A young legal tyro might find profit as well as entertainment in carefully studying others of Mr Skimpin's adroit methods in cross-examination. They are in a manner typical of those in favour with the more experienced members of the profession, allowing, of course, for a little humorous exaggeration. He will note also that Boz shows clearly how effective was the result of the processes. Here are a few useful recipes.

How to make a witness appear as though he wished to withhold the truth. How to highly discredit a witness by an opening question. How to insinuate inaccuracy. How to suggest that the witness is evading. How to deal with a statement of a particular number of instances. How to take advantage of a witness' glances. How to suggest another imputed meaning to a witness' statement and confuse him into accepting it.

Another happy and familiar form is Skimpin's interrogation of Winkle as to his 'friends'.

'Are they here?'

'Yes they are,' said Mr Winkle, *looking very earnestly towards the spot where his friends were stationed.*

As everyone attending courts knows, this is an almost intuitive movement in a witness; he thinks it corroborates him somehow.

But how good, Skimpin, and how ready.

'Pray attend to me, Mr Winkle, and *never mind your friends*,' with another expressive look at the jury; '*they must tell their stories without any previous consultation with you*, if none has yet taken place,' another expressive look. 'Now Sir, tell what you saw,' etc. '*Come, out with it, sir, we must have it sooner or later.*'

The assumption here that the witness would keep back what he knew is adroit and very convincing.

But now we come to a very critical passage in Mr Pickwick's case: one that really destroyed any chance that he had. It really settled the matter with the jury; and the worst was, the point was brought out through the inefficiency of his own counsel.

But let us hear the episode, and see how the foolish Phunky muddled it.

'I believe, Mr Winkle,' said Mr Phunky, 'that Mr Pickwick is not a young man?'

'Oh, no,' replied Mr Winkle; 'old enough to be my father.'

'You have told my learned friend that you have known Mr Pickwick a long time. Had you ever any reason to suppose or believe that he was about to be married?'

'Oh, no; certainly not,' replied Mr Winkle with so much eagerness, that Mr Phunky ought to have got him out of the box with all possible dispatch. Lawyers hold that there are two kinds of particularly bad witnesses – a reluctant witness, and a too-willing witness; it was Mr Winkle's fate to figure in both characters.

'I will even go further than this, Mr Winkle,' continued Mr Phunky, in a most smooth and complacent manner. 'Did you ever see anything in Mr Pickwick's manner and conduct towards the opposite sex, to induce you to believe that he ever contemplated matrimony of late years, in any case?'

'Oh, no; certainly not,' replied Mr Winkle.

'Has his behaviour, when females have been in the case, always been that of a man, who, having attained a pretty advanced period of life, content with his own occupations and amusements, treats them only as a father might his daughters?'

'Not the least doubt of it,' replied Mr Winkle, in the fulness of his heart. 'That is – yes – oh, yes – certainly.'

'You have never known anything in his behaviour towards Mrs Bardell, or any other female, in the least degree suspicious?' said Mr Phunky, preparing to sit down; for Serjeant Snubbin was winking at him.

'N-n-no,' replied Mr Winkle, 'except on one trifling occasion, which, I have no doubt, might be easily explained.'

Now, if the unfortunate Mr Phunky had sat down when Serjeant Snubbin had winked at him, or if Serjeant Buzfuz had stopped this irregular cross-examination at the outset (which he knew better than to do; observing Mr Winkle's anxiety, and well knowing it would, in all probability, lead to something serviceable to him), this unfortunate admission would not have been elicited. The moment the words fell from Mr Winkle's lips, Mr Phunky sat down, and Serjeant Snubbin rather hastily told him he might leave the box, which Mr Winkle prepared to do with great readiness, when Serjeant Buzfuz stopped him.

'You hear what the learned counsel says, Sir,' observed the judge, turning to the miserable and agonised Mr Winkle. 'Describe the occasion to which you refer.'

'My Lord,' said Mr Winkle, trembling with anxiety, 'I–I'd rather not.'

And Winkle had to relate the whole Ipswich adventure of the double-bedded room and the spinster lady.

It is surprising that Dodson and Fogg did not ferret out all about Mr Pickwick's adventure at the Great White Horse. Peter Magnus lived in town and must have heard of the coming case; these things *do* somehow leak out, and he would have gladly volunteered the story, were it only to spite the man. But further, Dodson and Fogg must have made all sorts of enquiries into Mr Pickwick's doings. Mrs Bardell herself might have heard something. The story was certainly in the Ipswich papers, for there was the riot in the street, the appearance before the mayor, the exposure of 'Captain FitzMarshall' – a notable business altogether. What a revelation in open court! Conceive Miss Witherfield called to depose to Mr Pickwick's midnight invasion. Mr Pickwick himself might have been called and put on the rack, this incident not concerning his breach of promise. And supposing that the ubiquitous Jingle had heard of this business and had gone to the solicitor's office to volunteer evidence, and most useful evidence it would have been – to wit that Mr Pickwick had been caught in the garden of a young ladies' school and had alarmed the house by his attempts to gain admission in the small hours! Jingle, of course, could not be permitted to testify to this, but he could put the firm on the track. Mr Pickwick's reputation could hardly have survived these two revelations, and sweeping damages to the full amount would have been the certain result.

This extraordinary adventure of Mr Pickwick's at the Great White Horse Inn, Ipswich, verifies Dodson's casual remark to him, that 'he was either a very designing or a most unfortunate man', circumstances being so strong against him. As the story was brought out, in open court, owing to the joint indiscretion of Phunky and Winkle, it will be best, in justice to Mr Pickwick, to give practically his account of the affair.

'Nobody sleeps in the other bed, of course,' said Mr Pickwick.

'Oh, no, Sir.'

'Very good. Tell my servant to bring me up some hot water at half-past eight in the morning, and that I shall not want him any more to-night.'

'Yes, Sir,' and bidding Mr Pickwick good night, the chambermaid retired, and left him alone.

Mr Pickwick sat himself down in a chair before the fire, and fell into a train of rambling meditations. First he thought of his friends, and wondered when they would join him; *then his mind reverted to Mrs Martha Bardell*; and from that lady it wandered, by a natural process, to the dingy counting-house of Dodson and Fogg. From Dodson and Fogg's it flew off at a tangent, to the very centre of the history of the queer client; and then it came back to the Great White Horse at Ipswich, with sufficient clearness to convince Mr Pickwick that he was falling asleep: so he aroused himself, and began to undress, when he recollected he had left his watch on the table downstairs.

So as it was pretty late now, and he was unwilling to ring his bell at that hour of the night, he slipped on his coat, of which he had just divested himself, and taking the japanned candlestick in his hand, walked quietly down stairs.

The more stairs Mr Pickwick went down, the more stairs there seemed to be to descend, and again and again, when Mr Pickwick got into some narrow passage, and began to congratulate himself on having gained the ground-floor, did another flight of stairs appear before his astonished eyes. At last he reached a stone hall, which he remembered to have seen when he entered the house. Passage after passage did he explore; room after room did he peep into; at length, just as he was on the point of giving up the search in despair, he opened the door of the identical room in which he had spent the evening, and beheld his missing property on the table.

Mr Pickwick seized the watch in triumph, and proceeded to retrace his steps to his bed-chamber. If his progress downwards had been attended with difficulties and uncertainty, his journey back was infinitely more perplexing. Rows of doors, garnished with boots of every shape, make, and size, branched off in every possible direction. A dozen times did he softly turn the handle of some bedroom door, which resembled his own, when a gruff cry from within of 'Who the devil's that?' or 'What do you want here?' caused him to steal away on tiptoe, with a perfectly marvellous celerity. He was reduced to the verge of despair, when an open door attracted his attention. He peeped in – right at last. There were the two beds, whose situation he perfectly remembered, and the fire still burning. His candle, not a long one when he first received it, had flickered away in the drafts of air through which he had passed, and sunk into the socket, just as he had closed the door after him. 'No matter,' said Mr Pickwick, 'I can undress myself just as well by the light of the fire.'

The bedsteads stood, one each side of the door; and on the inner side of each, was a little path, terminating in a rush-bottomed chair, just wide enough to admit of a person's getting into, or out of bed, on that side if he or she thought proper. Having carefully drawn the curtains of his bed on the outside, Mr Pickwick sat down on the rush-bottomed chair, and leisurely divested himself of his shoes and gaiters. He then took off and folded up, his coat, waistcoat, and neck-cloth, and slowly drawing on his tasselled nightcap, secured it firmly on his head, by tying beneath his chin, the strings which he always had attached to that article of dress. It was at this moment that the absurdity of his recent bewilderment struck upon his mind;

and throwing himself back in the rush-bottomed chair, Mr Pickwick laughed to himself so heartily, that it would have been quite delightful to any man of well-constituted mind to have watched the smiles which expanded his amiable features, as they shone forth, from beneath the night-cap.

'It is the best idea,' said Mr Pickwick to himself, smiling till he almost cracked the night-cap strings – 'It is the best idea, my losing myself in this place, and wandering about those staircases, that I ever heard of. Droll, droll, very droll.' Here Mr Pickwick smiled again, a broader smile than before, and was about to continue the process of undressing, in the best possible humour, when he was suddenly stopped by a most unexpected interruption; to wit, the entrance into the room of some person with a candle, who, after locking the door, advanced to the dressing table, and set down the light upon it.

The smile that played upon Mr Pickwick's features, was instantaneously lost in a look of the most unbounded and wonder-stricken surprise. The person, whoever it was, had come so suddenly and with so little noise, that Mr Pickwick had had no time to call out, or oppose their entrance. Who could it be? A robber? Some evil-minded person who had seen him come upstairs with a handsome watch in his hand, perhaps. What was he to do!

The only way in which Mr Pickwick could catch a glimpse of his mysterious visitor with the least danger of being seen himself, was by creeping on to the bed, and peeping out from between the curtains on the opposite side. Keeping the curtains carefully closed with his hand, so that nothing more of him could be seen than his face and nightcap, and putting on his spectacles, he mustered up courage, and looked out.

Mr Pickwick almost fainted with horror and dismay. Standing before the dressing glass, was a middle-aged lady in yellow curl-papers, busily engaged in brushing what ladies call their 'back hair'. However the unconscious middle-aged lady came into that room, it was quite clear that she contemplated remaining there for the night; for she had brought a rushlight and shade with her, which with praiseworthy precaution against fire, she had stationed in a basin on the floor, where it was glimmering away, like a gigantic lighthouse, in a particularly small piece of water.

'Bless my soul,' thought Mr Pickwick, 'what a dreadful thing!'

'Hem!' said the lady; and in went Mr Pickwick's head with automaton-like rapidity.

'I never met with anything so awful as this,' thought poor Mr Pickwick, the cold perspiration starting in drops upon his nightcap. 'Never. This is fearful.'

It was quite impossible to resist the urgent desire to see what was going forward. So out went Mr Pickwick's head again. The prospect was worse than before. The middle-aged lady had finished arranging her hair; had carefully enveloped it, in a muslin nightcap with a small plaited border, and was gazing pensively on the fire.

'This matter is growing alarming' – reasoned Mr Pickwick with himself. 'I can't allow things to go on in this way. By the self-possession of that lady, it's clear to me that I must have come into the wrong room. If I call out, she'll alarm the house, but if I remain here, the consequences will be still more frightful.'

Mr Pickwick, it is quite unnecessary to say, was one of the most modest and delicate-minded of mortals. The very idea of exhibiting his nightcap to a lady, overpowered him, but he had tied those confounded strings in a knot, and do what he would, he couldn't get it off. The disclosure must be made. There was only one other way of doing it. He shrunk behind the curtains, and called out very loudly –

'Ha – hum.'

That the lady started at this unexpected sound was evident, by her falling up against the rushlight shade; that she persuaded herself it must have been the effect of imagination was equally clear, for when Mr Pickwick, under the impression that she had fainted away, stone-dead from fright, ventured to peep out again, she was gazing pensively on the fire as before.

'Most extraordinary female this,' thought Mr Pickwick, popping in again. 'Ha – hum.'

These last sounds, so like those in which, as legends inform us, the ferocious giant Blunderbore was in the habit of expressing his opinion that it was time to lay the cloth, were too distinctly audible, to be again mistaken for the workings of fancy.

'Gracious Heaven!' said the middle-aged lady, 'what's that!'

'It's – it's – only a gentleman, Ma'am,' said Mr Pickwick from behind the curtains.

'A gentleman!' said the lady with a terrific scream.

'It's all over,' thought Mr Pickwick.

'A strange man,' shrieked the lady. Another instant and the house would be alarmed. Her garments rustled as she rushed towards the door.

'Ma'am,' said Mr Pickwick, thrusting out his head, in the extremity of desperation, 'Ma'am.'

Now although Mr Pickwick was not actuated by any definite object in putting out his head, it was instantaneously productive of a good effect. The lady, as we have already stated, was near the door. She must pass it, to reach the staircase, and she would most undoubtedly have done so by this time, had not the sudden apparition of Mr Pickwick's nightcap driven her back, into the remotest corner of the apartment, where she stood, staring wildly at Mr Pickwick, while Mr Pickwick, in his turn, stared wildly at her.

'Wretch,' said the lady, covering her eyes with her hands, 'what do you want here.'

'Nothing, Ma'am, nothing whatever, Ma'am,' said Mr Pickwick, earnestly.

'Nothing!' said the lady, looking up.

'Nothing, Ma'am, upon my honour,' said Mr Pickwick, nodding his head so energetically, that the tassel of his nightcap danced again. 'I am almost ready to sink, Ma'am, beneath the confusion of addressing a lady in my nightcap (here the lady hastily snatched off hers), but I can't get it off, Ma'am' (here Mr Pickwick gave it a tremendous tug in proof of the statement). 'It is evident to me, Ma'am, now, that I have mistaken this bedroom for my own. I had not been here five minutes, Ma'am, when you suddenly entered it.'

'If this improbable story be really true, Sir,' said the lady, sobbing violently, 'you will leave it instantly.'

'I will, Ma'am, with the greatest pleasure,' replied Mr Pickwick.

'Instantly, Sir,' said the lady.

'Certainly, Ma'am,' interposed Mr Pickwick very quickly. 'Certainly, Ma'am. I – I – am very sorry, Ma'am,' said Mr Pickwick, making his appearance at the bottom of the bed, 'to have been the innocent occasion of this alarm and emotion; deeply sorry, Ma'am.'

The lady pointed to the door. One excellent quality of Mr Pickwick's character was beautifully displayed at this moment, under the most trying circumstances. Although he had hastily put on his hat over his nightcap, after the manner of the old patrol; although he carried his shoes and gaiters in his hand, and his coat and waistcoat over his arm, nothing could subdue his native politeness.

'I am exceedingly sorry, Ma'am,' said Mr Pickwick, bowing very low.

'If you are, Sir, you will at once leave the room,' said the lady.

'Immediately, Ma'am; this instant, Ma'am,' said Mr Pickwick, opening the door, and dropping both his shoes with a loud crash in so doing.

'I trust, Ma'am,' resumed Mr Pickwick, gathering up his shoes, and turning round to bow again, 'I trust, Ma'am, that my unblemished character, and the devoted respect I entertain for your sex, will plead as some slight excuse for this' – But before Mr Pickwick could conclude the sentence, the lady had thrust him into the passage, and locked and bolted the door behind him.

Whatever grounds of self-congratulation Mr Pickwick might have, for having escaped so quietly from his late awkward situation, his present position was by no means enviable. He was alone, in an open passage, in a strange house, in the middle of the night, half dressed; it was not to be supposed that he could find his way in perfect darkness to a room which he had been wholly unable to discover with a light, and if he made the slightest noise in his fruitless attempts to do so, he stood every chance of being shot at, and perhaps killed, by some wakeful traveller. He had no resource but to remain where he was, until daylight appeared. So after groping his way a few paces down the passage, and to his infinite alarm, stumbling over several pairs of boots in so doing, Mr Pickwick crouched into a little recess in the wall, to wait for morning, as philosophically as he might.

He was not destined, however, to undergo this additional trial of patience: for he had not been long ensconced in his present concealment when, to his unspeakable horror, a man, bearing a light, appeared at the end of the passage. His horror was suddenly converted into joy, however, when he recognised the form of his faithful attendant. It was indeed Mr Samuel Weller, who after sitting up thus late, in conversation with the Boots, who was sitting up for the mail, was now about to retire to rest.

Imagine this story told by Miss Witherfield in open court, with all its details, the lady's narrative being coloured by the recollection that she had lost a suitable husband owing to her adventure. Mr Peter Magnus would have deposed to Mr Pickwick's extraordinary interest in the matter of the proposal, and have added his suspicions on recalling Mr Pickwick's ambiguous declaration that he had come down to expose a certain person – even one of his own sympathetic friends, who had witnessed the scene with Mrs Bardell, and recalled the boarding house incident, might murmur, 'How odd that he is ever thus in pursuit of the fair under suspicious circumstances? *could* it be that after all? – What if he had some previous knowledge of the lady, and secretly admired her, and stung to fury at the notion of Mr Peter Magnus marrying, had taken this strange mode of declaring his passion?' Even the sagacious Sam, devoted as he was to his master, was taken aback on meeting him in his midnight wanderings.

'Sam,' said Mr Pickwick, suddenly appearing before him, 'Where's my bedroom?'

Mr Weller stared at his master with the most emphatic surprise; and it was not until the question had been repeated three several times, that he turned round, and led the way to the long-sought apartment.

'Sam,' said Mr Pickwick, as he got into bed, 'I have made one of the most extraordinary mistakes to-night, that ever were heard of.'

'Werry likely, Sir,' replied Mr Weller, drily.

'But of this I am determined, Sam,' said Mr Pickwick, 'that if I were to stop in this house for six months, I would never trust myself about it alone, again.'

'That's the werry prudentest resolution as you could come to, Sir,' replied Mr Weller. 'You rayther want some-body to look arter you, Sir, ven your judgment goes out a wisitin'.'

'What do you mean by that, Sam?' said Mr Pickwick. He raised himself in bed, and extended his hand, as if he were about to say something more; but suddenly checking himself, turned round, and bade his valet 'Good night'.

'Good night, Sir,' replied Mr Weller. He paused when he got outside the door – shook his head – walked on – stopped – snuffed the candle – shook his head again – and finally proceeded slowly to his chamber, apparently buried in the profoundest meditation.

It will be seen that Sam went near to being disrespectful in his sceptical view of his master's story

When Mrs Sanders was examined, 'the court' put a few questions to her, as to the customs of love-making among persons of her position. She had 'received love letters, like other ladies. In the course of their correspondence Mr Sanders had often called her a "duck" but never "chops" or "tomato sauce". He was particularly fond of ducks. Perhaps if he had been as fond of chops and tomato sauce, he might have called her that, as a term of affection.'

Mrs Sanders was clearly one of the same class as Mrs Cluppins, and chiefly deposed to the general impression in the neighbourhood that Mr Pickwick had 'offered' for Mrs Bardell. Tupman, Snodgrass and Sam were also examined. Being friends of the defendant, they were from the outset assumed to be 'hostile' and treated accordingly. It may be doubted, however, whether it is permissible to treat 'your own witnesses' in this rough fashion, until at least they have shown some overt signs of their hostility, either by reserve, or an obvious determination to let as little as possible be extracted from them. In such cases, it is usual to apply to the court for its sanction to deal with them by the severity of cross-examination.

When Sam entered the witness box, the Serjeant addressed him: 'I believe you are in the service of Mr Pickwick, the Defendant in this case. *Speak up, if you please, Mr Weller.*' Sam had not had time to say anything, so the admonition might seem superfluous. But this is a well-known device. Sam had been 'briefed' to the Serjeant as a rather dangerous witness – somewhat too wide awake. It was necessary therefore to be short and summary with him. He thus conveyed to the jury that this Sam was one whom he could address in this curt way, and who by his low, uncertain accents might try to hide the truth. Sam, however, disconcerted the plan by his prompt, ready answer, 'I *mean* to speak up, sir.' Sam, as we know, clearly brought out Dodson and Fogg's damaging assurance to Mrs Bardell that no costs should be charged to her personally.

When the plaintiff's case was closed, things did not look particularly bright for Mr Pickwick. It had been shown on the evidence of his own friends that (1) he had been surprised with his landlady in his arms; (2) that he had been corresponding with her on most familiar terms – at least Serjeant Buzfuz had made it appear so; (3) language that *almost* amounted to a proposal had been overheard; (4) and finally, it had been revealed that the defendant had been 'caught' in a lady's bedroom, at an inn, at midnight! To answer which a 'strong' case was absolutely essential. This, we grieve to say, was not forthcoming.

THE DEFENDANT'S CASE

When we listen to the defence set up for Mr Pickwick we have to lament that that worthy gentleman was not better served by his legal advisers.

On the other side the shrewd Dodson and Fogg had done admirably for their client. They were sharp, clever attorneys, having a thundering, overpowering leader, and a smart, exceedingly smart junior, one of those 'wide-awake' brisk fellows who really conduct the case, and will 'take silk' in a few years. This gentleman could cross-examine in capital style and address the jury in a language of his own, by glances, shrugs, and remarks addressed to a witness, but intended for the jury, as they knew perfectly well. His style, bearing, and speeches form an admirable epitome of the arts and devices of a smart counsel. These are 'common' forms and Skimpin had them at his fingers' ends. As we listen, we feel how admirably directed they were to work on the jury.

Perker's plan of campaign as announced to Mr Pickwick, was a poor one enough, and showed how desperate he thought the case was. 'We have only one (course) to adopt, my dear sir,' he said, 'cross-examine the witnesses: trust to Snubbin's eloquence, throw dust in the eyes of the judge, and ourselves on the jury.' Brave words, but nothing of the programme was carried out. The cross-examination of the witnesses was but tamely attempted. Snubbin's eloquence was not displayed beyond mildly praising his client's good character. As for 'throwing dust in the eyes of the judge', we have seen Mr Justice Stareleigh was much too wide awake for that; while the throwing themselves on the jury was disastrous. There were several other lines of defence which a more up-to-date solicitor would not have overlooked. A less scrupulous man would have made searching enquiries into Mrs Bardell's history and character; but his client, perhaps, would not have sanctioned this course.

Perker is even absurd enough to talk of a *casa*, as though it were some Italian word.

A *ca sa* was short for a writ of *Capias ad Satisfaciendum*, which gave a warrant to the officers to seize the goods. There were various kinds of this machinery, but what affected Mr Pickwick was a *Capias ad Satisfaciendum*, to enforce attendance at the court. The *ca sa* also came after judgment, giving authority to imprison the defendant till the claim was satisfied.

The appearance of such great guns as the two Serjeants is accounted for by a curious rule that Serjeants only were permitted to lead in cases read in the Court of Common Pleas.* This strange monopoly recalls that other one, in the Court of Arches, where the advocates and judges used to exchange places and decide on cases in which perhaps they had been advocates. These illiberal and unaccountable restrictions have been swept away, with the courts themselves.

Very unusual indeed at this time was the appearance of a lawyer of Serjeant Snubbin's class in court, and there is a well-known story how, when Charles Butler made his appearance on a special occasion, all the Bar crowded in to hear him, and he had, I think, to get a gown for the occasion.

One is sorry to think that there are no Serjeants now, though at the Irish Bar there is one solitary survivor – Serjeant Hemphill. Gone, too, are their 'coifs' and other paraphernalia. With the abolition of the separate courts they were found

* Seven years after the trial this monopoly was taken away from the Serjeants – namely in 1834: then capriciously given back to them, and finally abolished in 1840.

superfluous. We like to hear of Serjeant Parry, Serjeant Ballantine, Serjeants Warren and Talfourd, all four literary men.*

Having made this initial blunder, Perker did not even instruct a good, smart and ready junior, but chose instead the incapable Phunky who really brought out that fatal piece of evidence from Winkle, which 'did for' his case altogether. He had no business, as Boz tells us.

This junior, we are told, had been just called, that is to say, he had been only eight years at the Bar. Snubbin had never heard of him. The little judge, in court, also said 'that he never had the pleasure of hearing the gentleman's name before', a sneer he would not have ventured on to a counsel in good practice. Snubbin's remark is amusing and sarcastic; but nowadays any barrister who had been at the Bar eight years would not be considered as 'just called', for if he has been passed over for that time, he is likely never to make a figure. The rude and unbecoming sneers, both of Snubbin and the little judge, seem amazing in our present code of legal manners. Everything at that time, however, was much more 'in the rough' and coarser. This was his first case; and the poor creature is thus described:

Although an infant barrister, he was a full-grown man. He had a very nervous manner, and a painful hesitation in his speech; it did not appear to be a natural defect, but seemed rather the result of timidity, arising from the consciousness of being 'kept down' by want of means, or interest, or

* I have heard from the daughter of Mr Chapman, the original publisher of *Pickwick*, that Talfourd revised and directed the 'trial'. On one occasion Boz was dining with him when the proof was brought in, with some legal mistakes by Talfourd. Boz left the table and put it right.

connection, or impudence, as the case might be. He was overawed by the Serjeant, and profoundly courteous to the attorney.

'I have not had the pleasure of seeing you before, Mr Phunky,' said Serjeant Snubbin, with haughty condescension.

Mr Phunky bowed. He *had* had the pleasure of seeing the Serjeant, and of envying him too, with all a poor man's envy, for eight years and a quarter.

'You are with me in this case, I understand?' said the Serjeant.

If Mr Phunky had been a rich man, he would have instantly sent for his clerk to remind him; if he had been a wise one, he would have applied his fore-finger to his forehead, and endeavoured to recollect, whether, in the multiplicity of his engagements he had undertaken this one, or not; but as he was neither rich nor wise (in this sense at all events) he turned red, and bowed.

'Have you read the papers, Mr Phunky?' inquired the Serjeant.

Here again, Mr Phunky should have professed to have forgotten all about the merits of the case; but as he had read such papers as had been laid before him in the course of the action, and had thought of nothing else, waking or sleeping, throughout the two months during which he had been retained as Mr Serjeant Snubbin's junior, he turned a deeper red, and bowed again.

'This is Mr Pickwick,' said the Serjeant, waving his pen in the direction in which that gentleman was standing.

Mr Phunky bowed to Mr Pickwick with a reverence which a first client must ever awaken; and again inclined his head towards his leader.

'Perhaps you will take Mr Pickwick away,' said the Serjeant, 'and – and – and – hear anything Mr Pickwick may wish to communicate. We shall have a consultation, of course.' With this hint that he had been interrupted quite long enough, Mr Serjeant Snubbin, who had been gradually growing more and more abstracted, applied his glass to his eyes for an instant, bowed slightly round, and was once more deeply immersed in the case before him: which arose out of an interminable law suit, originating in the act of an individual, deceased a century or so ago, who had stopped up a pathway leading from some place which nobody ever came from, to some other place which nobody ever went to.

With such a pair the case was literally given away. Perker should have secured a man like the present Mr Gill or Mr Charles Matthews – they might have 'broken down' the witnesses, or laughed the case out of court.

We may speculate why did Perker make this foolish selection? As to Snubbin there was some excuse, as it was the custom that Serjeants only should lead in the Court of Common Pleas. But for the choice of Phunky, Perker's stupidity alone was responsible.

Under these conditions Serjeant Snubbin's conduct of the case and his 'handling' of the witnesses was truly inefficient. He lost every opportunity for helping his client. He 'led' in a quiet, gentlemanly and almost indifferent way. His first opportunity came in examining Mrs Cluppins. As we have seen, she had deposed to hearing, when the door was 'on the jar', Mr Pickwick make those speeches which Mrs Bardell had taken to be a proposal. Now here was the moment to show the ambiguity and that Mr Pickwick was speaking of his servant. It might have been brought out that Sam was actually engaged that day, and that she had met him on the stairs, etc. But Snubbin declined to ask her a single question, saying that Mr Pickwick admitted the accuracy of her statement. But this was beside the matter, and the Serjeant need not have impeached her accuracy.

When Phunky came to Winkle, the inexperience of the tyro was shown at once. Again, here was the moment to have extracted from the witness a full explanation of Mr Pickwick's ambiguous speeches to Mrs Bardell. He could have 'brought out' as 'clear as the light of day' that Mr Pickwick was speaking of his engagement of a valet and have shown that the valet was to be engaged that very morning. It would have been impossible to resist such an explanation. But the thing was not thought of. From him also could have been drawn a vast deal favourable to Mr Pickwick such as his disgust and annoyance at Mrs Bardell's behaviour, his wish to be rid of her, his complaints of her conduct. But no, there was only the foolish question as to Mr Pickwick's being an elderly man and of fatherly ways, a topic that would by no means negative the presumption of matrimony. But nothing could excuse the rashness of putting a general question as to 'Mr Pickwick's behaviour towards females'. No adroit counsel would run the risk of encountering a too conscientious witness, such as Winkle proved to be and who would 'let the cat out of the bag'.

As we have seen, this awkward question settled Mr Pickwick's business. Snubbin had held him out as an elderly but benevolent being, treating every female he met as a daughter, never dreaming of matrimony: when lo! the whole fabric is overthrown in an instant by the luckless Winkle's admission!

Amid the profound silence of the whole court Mr Winkle faltered out that the trifling circumstance of suspicion was

Mr Pickwick's being found in a lady's sleeping apartment at midnight, which had terminated, *he believed*, in breaking off the projected marriage of the lady, and had led, *he knew*, to the whole party being forcibly carried before a magistrate.

Thus was the defendant suddenly revealed as a Pecksniffian Lothario, and his pretence of philanthropy after was shown in its true colours. It was impossible not to associate this with the scene with Mrs Bardell.

But there was an important legal 'point' which one might have expected would have occurred to so eminent a chamber counsel as Serjeant Snubbin. To prove a breach of the promise, it must always be shown that the defendant had been given an opportunity of officially refusing to fulfil it. It should have been put to him 'in black and white', 'Will you marry me?' and he must have answered 'No, I will not,' or something to that effect. In default of this the defendant might plead: 'True I gave the promise and it stands unbroken, for you never required me to act upon it.' Now in Mr Pickwick's case this actually occurred. As we have seen he left town the morning after the imputed proposal and while he was away, within a month, the notice of action was sent to him. Up to that time he had not heard a word of Dodson and Fogg, or of legal proceedings. But it may be urged that Mrs Bardell herself may have written, formulating her demands. That this was not the case is evident from Mr Pickwick's behaviour; he did not dream of such a thing, or he would have been disturbed by it, or have consulted his friends about it. Had it been so, his high opinion of Mrs Bardell would have been shattered. For did he not say on seeing Dodson and Fogg's letter, 'She couldn't do it, she hasn't the heart to do it.' The only thing that makes against this theory is his reply to Peter Magnus who asked him 'had he ever proposed?' when he answered vehemently 'Never', possibly recalling Mrs Bardell. She may however have written to him a pleading letter reminding him of what he had said to her, declaring her deep-seated affection for him and inviting him to carry out what he had offered. Mr Pickwick would have replied in one of his amiable letters, couched in rather general terms, perhaps calling her 'my dear creature', but putting aside the whole business: and there the matter probably dropped for a time. I have little doubt the good woman up to the last really believed that her elderly lodger intended to make her an offer of his hand, and that on his return from his travels he would resume the business. Much elated by this prospect, and most naturally too, she had told all her friends and neighbours of her approaching advancement. This Mrs Sanders specially deposed to: 'had always said and believed that Pickwick would marry Mrs Bardell; knew that Mrs Bardell being engaged to Pickwick was the current topic of conversation in the neighbourhood, after the fainting in July; had been told it herself by Mrs Mudberry which kept a mangle, and Mrs Bunkin which clear-starched, but did not see either Mrs Mudberry or Mrs Bunkin in court.'

Notwithstanding these speculations, it still does not appear that Pickwick made such a legal and official refusal to execute his promise as would be sufficient to support the statement of what is now called 'the summons and plaint', to wit, that the plaintiff being able and willing 'to marry the defendant the defendant refused, etc'.

There is another matter on which hands of skilful counsel might have affected Mrs Bardell and which my friend Mr Burnand ('F.C.B.') was the first to push home. At the trial, Mrs Sanders, cross-examined by Serjeant Snubbin, had to admit that her friend had an admirer – a certain baker in the neighbourhood – who was supposed to have matrimonial designs. Pressed on this matter she thus deposed:

Had heard Pickwick ask the little boy how he should like to have another father. Did not know that Mrs Bardell was at that time keeping company with the baker, but did know that the baker was then a single man, and is now married. Couldn't swear that Mrs Bardell was not very fond of the baker, but should think that the baker was not very fond of Mrs Bardell, or he wouldn't have married somebody else. Thought Mrs Bardell fainted away on the morning in July, because Pickwick asked her to name the day; knew that she (witness) fainted away stone dead when Mr Sanders asked *her* to name the day, and believed that everybody as called herself a lady would do the same, under similar circumstances. Heard Pickwick ask the boy the question about the marbles, but upon her oath did not know the difference between an alley tor and a commoney.

By the Court.   During the period of her keeping company with Mr Sanders, had received love letters, like other ladies. In course of their correspondence Mr Sanders had often called her a 'duck', but never 'chops', nor yet 'tomata sauce'. He was particularly fond of ducks. Perhaps if he had been as fond of chops and tomata sauce, he might have called her that, as a term of affection.

What a point, too, Serjeant Snubbin missed here! Could he not have quoted the old verses. How he would have convulsed the court as he poured out the apropos 'for Tommy and Me'!

Pat-a-cake, Pat-a-cake, baker's man,
Bake me a cake as quick as you can;

Knead it and bake it as fast as can be,
And put in the oven for Tommy and me.

Now we do not find that the Serjeant made any use of this topic in his speech. He might have surely urged that this 'wily and experienced widow' was eager for a husband, that having been 'thrown over' by her baker and stung by the mortification, she resolved, as it were, to rehabilitate herself and prepare this 'plant' for her unsuspecting lodger. As Sir Henry Irving says in the play, 'I don't like widows; they know too much.' F.C.B., as I have said, has treated this baker theme and developed it regularly in his amusing operetta 'Pickwick'.

The little epitome given of Snubbin's speech shows how weak were his topics, and that he, in fact, considered that there was no defence.

Serjeant Snubbin then addressed the jury on behalf of the defendant; and a very long and a very emphatic address he delivered, in which he bestowed the highest possible eulogiums on the conduct and character of Mr Pickwick. He attempted to show that the letters which had been exhibited, merely related to Mr Pickwick's dinner, or to the preparations for receiving him in his apartments on his return from some country excursion. It is sufficient to add in general terms, that he did the best he could for Mr Pickwick; and the best, as everybody knows on the infallible authority of the old adage, could do no more. This was no more than speaking 'in mitigation of damages'.

Mr Phunky made no speech, which was just as well, as he might have but damaged the case, as no witnesses had been called on his side. For the same reason, the court had not the pleasure of hearing Skimpin, who would no doubt have 'torn the Defendant's case to tatters'.

The regular formula is this. The judge begins to read his notes, and makes 'running comments' as he goes along. 'We have first, gentlemen, the statement of Mrs Cluppins, she tells you, &c. Of course she comes as the friend of the plaintiff, and naturally takes a favourable view of her case. If you are satisfied with her statement, it is for you, gentlemen, to consider what value you will attach to it. Then we come to the question of damages. This is entirely a matter for you. You must take into account the position in life of the defendant, and what the plaintiff has lost by his default. On the other hand they must be reasonable in amount. If you believe the promise has been clearly established, you should give substantial though not excessive damages, on a scale sufficient to repay the plaintiff for the wrong. On the other hand – should it seem to you doubtful whether the promise had been made – you will give the defendant the benefit of the doubt. These are questions entirely for you – not for me. On the whole case, you will ask yourselves, whether a promise such as would satisfy reasonable men, has been supported by sufficient evidence. If so, plaintiff is entitled to damages – on the other hand, if this is not proved to your satisfaction, you will find for the defendant.'

Mr Justice Stareleigh, however, as we are told, then,

summed up in his old established and most approved form. He read as much of his notes as he could decypher on so short a notice, and made running comments on the evidence as he went along. If Mrs Bardell were right, it was perfectly clear that Mr Pickwick was wrong, and if they thought the evidence of Mrs Cluppins worthy of credence, they would believe it, and if they didn't, why they wouldn't.

If they were satisfied that a breach of promise had been committed, they would find for the Plaintiff, with such damages as they thought proper; and if, on the other hand, it appeared to them that no promise of marriage had ever been given, they would find for the Defendant, with no damages at all.

Such was this lucid direction – which is really, not in the least, an exaggeration.

But I could fancy some acute judge of our time – such as Mr Justice Day or Mr Justice Bigham – after trying this case, turning round in his seat to 'charge' the jury. 'Here, gentlemen,' he would tell them, 'we have it claimed on one side that a promise of marriage was made – and broken; on the other hand the defendant denies having ever given such a promise. The question you will have to deal with is: What was this promise, and when was it given? In other words, *when* did the defendant propose to the lady. On the part of the plaintiff, this was said to have been done at the interview in Goswell Street, and two friends of the plaintiff, Mrs Cluppins, I think' – turning over his notes – 'yes, Cluppins, and Sanders both declare positively that they overheard the language of the proposal. Further, Mr Pickwick's friends are called, to prove that the lady was in his arms, fainting. It is extraordinary that not one of these three gentlemen should have deposed to any statements or have offered explanations of the situation. One witness indeed says that he heard the defendant remonstrate with the plaintiff, on her hysterical behaviour, and ask her to consider that if anyone should come in, what would be said. Now, this is not the language of an ardent suitor, who would rather wish than otherwise, that such endearing familiarities should continue: though I don't think you need seriously accept the reading the learned counsel, Mr Skimpin, put on the phrase used; on the other hand, the words "my dear creature" were distinctly heard.

'There is one little incident,' the judge might go on, 'which I must not pass by, and which is not without its significance. A witness deposed that the defendant was noted for his kindness to the plaintiff's little boy – that he was constantly giving him presents, and once was heard to say to him, patting him on the head, "*how would you like to have another father?*" Now, this addressed to a child of tender years does seem an odd sort of speech. Of course, it will be contended that the reference was to the probability of his mother marrying someone other than the defendant: if that be the case, it seems to me rather an indelicate and reckless speech. And then it must be said, it seems inconsistent with the amiable and benevolent character given to the defendant today. On the other hand, if he were referring to *himself* it will appear natural and proper enough. And there is this to be added, that when the child had reported the remark to his mother, which of course he did, she would most reasonably begin to found hopes upon it. And then what follows, gentlemen? – the defendant is found holding this lady in his arms, and becomes so demonstrative in his attentions that this very child comes to her rescue. I am inexperienced in these things – they may be innocent and done with the purest intentions, or may not; but you, gentlemen of the jury, are men of the world: and it is for you to put the proper construction on them.

'You will have noted, gentlemen, this curious feature of the case. None of the witnesses were in the room when the imputed proposal was made, yet all, Cluppins, Weller, and the defendant's three friends, *heard* what the defendant said. This suggests that he must have been very pressing, if not agitated.

One of the witnesses, Winkle, I think, yes, Winkle, actually deposes to hearing the words, "My dear creature! Compose yourself" and the like. He added he was afraid someone might come in; a very reasonable fear, gentlemen, and well grounded: for several persons *did* come in and it would seem with awkward results for the defendant. But, gentlemen, I confess that what most of all weighs with me in this case is the remarkable avowal wrung from a reluctant witness, of the defendant's being surprised at midnight in a lady's bed-chamber, and being taken, after a serious riot, before the magistrates. This came on me, as I saw it did on you all, as a surprise. True, it does not bear on the question of a promise or of the breach. But still it seems a matter which you cannot wholly shut out from your consideration. It startled me as it did you, to find a sort of travelling philanthropist, as the defendant Pickwick holds himself out to be, on whose mildly benevolent features nature seems to have stamped rectitude and high principle, living a life of hypocrisy, taking part in midnight invasions and daylight riots. It is one of his own friends who tells us this sad story: and it is for you to consider whether the plaintiff was here also in pursuit of yet another disreputable game, holding out marriage as the bait: I seem to speak strongly, but I feel it would be impossible to withdraw this from your consideration.

'You may reasonably ask yourselves of what Pickwick was afraid – or why did he dread the presence of witnesses? Was he simply beguiling the lady, as he attempted to beguile that lady at Ipswich, without "meaning business", as the phrase runs. I must say the plaintiff had rather reasonable grounds for assuming that the defendant *did* mean business. But all this is for you, Gentlemen, not for me.

'Then we have the man Weller's statement – a sort of humorous stage servant, not unamusing – and of course entirely devoted to his master's interest. I don't think you need attach any importance to what he said of the solicitors for the plaintiff. When I was at the Bar, gentlemen, attorneys did much worse things than this.'

The jury consulted for only a few minutes. Perhaps, however, they were only discussing the amount of damages. They were certainly moderate – laid at £1,500 – though had Dodson and Fogg's advice prevailed, it should have been double. This only, by the way, is further proof of the amiable Mrs Bardell's moderation and secret *tendre* for her genial lodger. Considering that Mr Pickwick was 'a gentleman', and further a gentleman of means, and that Mrs Bardell was but an humble lodging-house keeper, the sum seems hardly commensurate. Dodson and Fogg no doubt expected £1,000.

An anxious quarter of an hour elapsed; the jury came back; the judge was fetched in. Mr Pickwick put on his spectacles, and gazed at the foreman with an agitated countenance and a quickly beating heart.

'Gentlemen,' said the individual in black, 'are you all agreed upon your verdict?'

'We are,' replied the foreman.

'Do you find for the plaintiff, gentlemen, or for the defendant?'

'For the plaintiff.'

'With what damages, gentlemen?'

'Seven hundred and fifty pounds.'

Mr Pickwick took off his spectacles, carefully wiped the glasses, folded them into their case, and put them in his pocket; then having drawn on his gloves with great nicety, and stared at the foreman all the while, he mechanically followed Mr Perker and the blue bag out of court.

They stopped in a side room while Perker paid the court fees; and here, Mr Pickwick was joined by his friends. Here, too, he encountered Messrs Dodson and Fogg, rubbing their hands with every token of outward satisfaction.

'Well, gentlemen,' said Mr Pickwick.

'Well, sir,' said Dodson: for self and partner.

'You imagine you'll get your costs, don't you, gentlemen?' said Mr Pickwick.

Fogg said they thought it rather probable. Dodson smiled, and said they'd try.

'You may try, and try, and try again, Messrs Dodson and Fogg,' said Mr Pickwick vehemently, 'but not one farthing of costs or damages do you ever get from me, if I spend the rest of my existence in a debtor's prison.'

'Ha, ha!' laughed Dodson. 'You will think better of that, before next term, Mr Pickwick.'

'He, he, he! We'll soon see about that, Mr Pickwick,' grinned Mr Fogg.

Speechless with indignation, Mr Pickwick allowed himself to be led by his solicitor and friends to the door, and there assisted into a hackney-coach, which had been fetched for the purpose, by the ever watchful Sam Weller.

Sam had put up the steps; and was preparing to jump upon the box, when he felt himself gently touched on the shoulder; and looking round, his father stood before him. The old gentleman's countenance wore a mournful expression, as he shook his head gravely, and said, in warning accents:

'I know'd what 'ud come 'o this here mode 'o doin' bisness. Oh Sammy, Sammy, vy worn't there a alleybi!'

We may wonder that the laborious Chamber Counsel Serjeant Snubbin did not advise 'moving for a new trial'. The verdict was clearly a wrong one – no sufficient evidence had been furnished either of a promise, or a breach. The full court would no doubt have granted the motion, and this would have led to Mr Pickwick's release, for the astute Dodson and Fogg must have recognised their poor chances, and perhaps have required 'security for costs', which their client could not have given. However, the idea did not occur to anybody.

Since the law was changed both plaintiff and defendant may be examined in such cases as these. What a different complexion this would have put on the suit. The whole case would have tumbled to pieces like a pack of cards. For Mr Pickwick 'put into the box' would have clearly shown that all that had been thus misconstrued, was his proposal for engaging a valet, which was to have been that very morning. He would have related the words of the dialogue, and the jury would have seen at once how the mistake arose. On the other hand, he would have been exposed to a severe rating cross-examination by the learned Serjeant – fortified by Winkle's most damaging slip about the White Horse incident – who would have forced out of him all the incidents. We can almost hear the Serjeant subject the defendant to the torture.

'This fellow of yours, Sir, was he recommended to you by a friend?'

'No – not at all.'

'By a Registry Office?'

'Certainly not – nothing of the kind.'

'Nothing of the kind? I suppose too low a class of place for you, eh? Come, Sir!'

'I never said such a thing.'

'Nor thought it, I suppose? Come, Sir, no beating about the bush. In plain terms, did you get him from a low Public House in the Boro'?'

Mr Pickwick started up.

'Never!'

'Do you deny it?'

'I never knew that the White Hart was a low Public House,' said the witness indignantly.

'Never mind what you know, Sir. Did you or did you not get him from there?' thundered the Serjeant.

'Of course I did.'

'Of course you did. Then what's the use of all this juggling. It does you no good with My Lord and the Jury. I tell you plainly, Mr Pickwick, we mean to have all out of you. Now Sir, was this man of yours an experienced valet?'

'Certainly not.'

'He had, of course, some training in his profession in other families?'

'Not that I know of.'

'Not that you know of. Do you dare to persist in that, Sir?'

'Why not?'

'Don't ask *me* questions, Sir, I'm asking *you*. Do you deny, Sir, that the man was neither more nor less than a common Boots in the yard of a Public House, wearing an old tattered hat and jacket – very different from the suit in which you have rigged him up here to-day?'

Mr Pickwick was astonished and silent. He was suffering. He had never dreamed of this view.

'Why,' he said, 'I suppose –'

'We want none of your supposes, Sir, answer yes or no.'

'Well, he certainly was such as you describe.'

A flutter ran round the court.

'And this creature of yours, you would impose on the Jury as a trained manservant. You may go down, Sir.'

This famous firm of city attorneys has become a byword in legal history – being considered the most notorious of practitioners for sharp, underhand, scheming practices. Boz was always vehement against the abuses of the law, but his generous ardour sometimes led him to exaggerated and wholesale statements that were scarcely well founded. This is found in some degree even in the sweeping attacks in *Bleak House*. But he was so vivid, so persuasive, in his pictures, that there was no appeal.

The unreasoning fury of Mr Pickwick is specially shown in the case of Jingle, whom he pursued with an animosity that was almost frantic. One would think it was some public enemy he was hunting down for the public good. Poor Jingle had really done nothing so monstrous, after all. He had 'chaffed' Dr Slammer, 'run off' with the spinster aunt – nothing so uncommon in those days – had been consigned to the Fleet for non-payment of his debts, and there showed penitence and other signs of a good heart. His one serious offence was passing himself off as a naval officer, and under an assumed name. But he had *crossed* Mr Pickwick – had ridiculed him – had contemptuously sent a message to 'Tuppy'. When he dared to play a practical joke on his persecutor, his infamy passed beyond bounds. Here was the key to Mr Pickwick's nature – any lack of homage or respect was an offence against morality. So with Dodson and Fogg. He had settled in his mind that a condescending visit to these gentlemen, with a little explanation and remonstrance, would completely disarm them. His fury on his advances being rejected was extraordinary.

Here Boz shows, as he ever does, his profound and most logical treatment of human character. He never goes astray, being guided by a happy and true instinct. Mr Pickwick had grown to be the most inflated of men. Flattered and followed – submitted to with the greatest deference – ordering people about – doing what he pleased – he could not stand the slightest opposition. No one was to contradict – no one to question even his stockings – speckled or others. Even when he was clearly wrong, it was an affront to hint at it. He had much in common with that great man, Mr Gladstone, who was the political Pickwick of his time. He was overbearing and arrogant and unrestrained, and I am afraid vindictive. Dodson and Fogg were associated with the great mortification of his life. He could not forgive them – the very sight of them roused his hatred, and the having to pay them ransom stung him to fury. All which is most natural and yet unexpected.

The popular and genial Sir Frank Lockwood was almost the first to put forward a plea in abatement of prejudice for the firm. He showed that they were not much below the usual type of middle-class solicitors. What they did was in the ordinary course. With Mr Pickwick they were most forbearing, and even indulgent. There was one rather doubtful passage, but even here he offers extenuation. This was their treatment of poor Ramsey, which, at first sight, seems very bad indeed.

'There was such a game with Fogg here, this mornin',' said the man in the brown coat, 'while Jack was upstairs sorting the papers, and you two were gone to the stamp-office. Fogg was down here opening the letters, when that chap we issued the writ against at Camberwell, you know, came in – what's his name again?'

'Ramsey,' said the clerk who had spoken to Mr Pickwick.

'Ah, Ramsey – a precious seedy-looking customer. "Well, sir," says old Fogg, looking at him very fierce – you know his way – "well, Sir, have you come to settle?" "Yes, I have, Sir," said Ramsey, putting his hand in his pocket, and bringing out the money, "the debt two pound ten, and the costs three pound five, and here it is, sir;" and he sighed like bricks, as he lugged out the money, done up in a bit of blotting paper. Old Fogg looked first at the money, and then at him, and then he coughed in his rum way, so that I knew something was coming. "You don't know there's a declaration filed, which increases the costs materially, I suppose?" said Fogg. "You don't say that, Sir," said Ramsey, starting back; "the time was only out last night, Sir." "I do say it, though," said Fogg, "my clerk's just gone to file it. Hasn't Mr Jackson gone to file that declaration in Bullman and Ramsey, Mr Wicks?" Of course I said yes, and then Fogg coughed again, and looked at Ramsey. "My God!" said Ramsey; "and here have I nearly driven myself mad, scraping this money together, and all to no purpose." "None at all," said Fogg, coolly; "so you had better go back and scrape some more together, and bring it here in time." "I can't get it, by God," said Ramsey, striking the desk with his fist. "Don't bully me, Sir," said Fogg, getting into a passion on purpose. "I am not bullying you, Sir," said Ramsey. "You are," said Fogg; "get out, Sir, get out of this office, Sir, and come back, Sir, when you know how to behave yourself." Well, Ramsey tried to speak, but Fogg wouldn't let him, so he put the money in his pocket, and sneaked out. The door was scarcely shut, when old Fogg turned round to me, with a sweet smile on his face, and drew the declaration out of his coat pocket. "Here, Wicks," says Fogg, "take a cab, and go down to the Temple as quick as you can, and file that. The costs are quite safe, for he's a steady man with a large family, at a salary of five-and-twenty shillings a week, and if he gives us a warrant of attorney, as he must in the end, I know his employers will see it paid; so we may as well get all we can out of him, Mr Wicks; it's a Christian act to do it, Mr Wicks, for with his large family and small income, he'll be all the better for a good lesson against getting into debt, – won't he, Mr Wicks, won't he?" – and he smiled so good-naturedly as he went away, that it was delightful to see him. He is a capital man of business,' said Wicks, in a tone of the deepest admiration, 'capital, isn't he?'

The other three cordially subscribed to this opinion, and the anecdote afforded the most unlimited satisfaction.

'Nice men these here, Sir,' whispered Mr Weller to his master; 'wery nice notion of fun they has, Sir.'

Sir F. Lockwood, by the way, offers one of the most amusing proofs conceivable, of the convincing power of 'Pickwick', which is constantly taking us out of the world of fiction, into that of the daily living life. He speaks of the cruel trick played upon the unfortunate Ramsey, who came to pay his bill of costs, and was told that these were out of date, had been swelled by subsequent proceedings. An affidavit had been sworn – which, after he left the house, Wicks, the clerk, was sent off to swear – then, Sir Frank adds: 'After all, this is merely given *as the statement of Wicks – on whose testimony not much reliance can be placed.*' As though Wicks were some living witness, 'erect upon two legs', whom he had been examining in court!

It must, however, be recollected that this was an *ex-parte* story. Wicks, as Sir F. Lockwood hints, may have coloured it up, to amuse his brethren. The truth is these poor helpless debtors, who fall into the hands of legal 'sharks' and money-lenders, have *their* tricks also. They will often 'do' those they employ if they can. And further, let this be considered. Before

Ramsey paid his visit the affidavit *had* been prepared, and was actually in Fogg's pocket. Such affidavit would not be allowed for in the costs unless necessary to the case, so that Fogg's statement that it had been filed was very near the truth. Perker himself was playing the same game of hide and seek with another unfortunate – one Watty – who was trying to see him, and learn something about his case, but was always put off with the excuse or falsehood, that Perker was out, though he was within. But then, 'Perker was an honourable man.'

Boz lets us know, through Sam, how the case reached Dodson and Fogg. He speaks of 'the kind generous people o' "the perfession" as sets their clerks to work to find out little disputes among their neighbours and acquaintances as wants settlin' by means of law suits.' This system, however, cannot be checked, and 'the speculative attorney' even in our time still flourishes.

It was really not a question whether Mr Pickwick would 'indict them for a conspiracy', because they acted as solicitors against him, but whether they would bring an action against *him* on their own account. All through, Mr Pickwick's behaviour to them had been outrageous. He chose to assume, quite gratuitously, that it was they – not Mrs Bardell – who got up the case; that they had worked on her for their own nefarious ends. Nothing could be more absurd. The landlady was eager enough to protect her own interests – her female friends worked on her, and the loss of so valuable a lodger, which the incident must have entailed, inflamed her more. We can see from Sam's interview with her that she was at last, though at first reluctant, determined to have her rights. But Mr Pickwick acting on this assumption addressed the firm, from the first to the last, in the most scurrilous language. He called them 'robbers, swindlers, – a brace of pettifogging scoundrels!'

Shocking and ungentlemanly terms, and what is worse, actionable. Yet the pair received this abuse with infinite good temper and restraint, merely securing a witness who should listen, and threatening the speaker with legal penalties.

And why did they not take this course? Well, they had to suspend proceedings until Mrs Bardell's action was settled, when on receiving their costs they were desirous to part in good humour. But Mr Pickwick was so furious at being invited to shake hands with them, that he again broke out with coarse abuse, 'Robbers! Robbers!' calling it after them down the stairs. Why did they not take action on this? Perhaps they were afraid; as Mr Pickwick had shown himself such a doughty and unyielding fighter – going to prison rather than pay. Perhaps they thought he might get the better of them again.

We have very little evidence as to what was the scale of fees in use in those days. They were of course far lower than they are now, after allowances even for the lower cost of living. Today, the fees to counsel alone would have absorbed considerably more than Dodson and Fogg's whole bill of costs. A nice point is, could Mr Pickwick's irregular interview with Serjeant Snubbin be considered something in the way of a consultation? Here were counsel, solicitor and client: the Serjeant gave up a portion of his valuable time and, further, the junior counsel was summoned specially from his chambers to supply his 'advice and opinion'. Mr Pickwick ought surely to have to pay for his whim.

And the bill of costs that these 'sharks' of attorneys sent in! It was astonishingly moderate. For writ, service of subpoenas, hunting up evidence, consultation, fees to counsel, fees for the day, retainers, etc. – the sum of £120 was all that was asked.

Imagine Messrs Lewis and Lewis sending in such a demand at the end of a trial which it had taken them nearly a year to get ready. In our time it could hardly be done under £1,000. Perker, by the way, told his client that on payment of the costs both of plaintiff and defendant, into the hands of 'these sharks' he would get his release. With much indulgence the attorneys allowed him to leave the prison on his bare undertaking to pay. And it is not clear why he should pay his own costs to them, and not to Perker. And they were *not* paid for some time. Mr Pickwick's own costs must have been small. He had no witnesses. Perker would not have made a hand of him, and I fancy he would have got off for £90, or £100. There were, however, the fees of the special jury, so he would have to pay, say, £220.

Perker, it has been shown, was not a very brilliant solicitor, and his views on the trial were somewhat cloudy. When he was urging his client to leave the Fleet he threw out some equally shadowy and ill-informed notions as to what might be done in the way of punishing the nefarious solicitors, Dodson and Fogg, 'those Freeman's Court Sharks'.

His great charge was that they had got a cognovit, or undertaking to pay their costs out of Mrs Bardell – their own client! Mr Pickwick refused to pay them – why should not she? The poor woman had 'blabbed' to Sam, a careless and natural assurance of theirs, that they would be content to get them from Mr Pickwick – a thing many a firm would do. But Perker here sees a regular conspiracy. 'I cannot undertake to say whether the wording of the cognovit, the nature of the ostensible consideration and the proof we can get together about the whole conduct of the suit, *will be sufficient to justify an indictment for conspiracy.*'

It is impossible to understand this bit of legal jargon. (1) 'The wording of the cognovit' – one could speculate on that without seeing it. (2) 'The nature of the ostensible consideration' was not far to seek – it being work and labour done for the plaintiff. And again, supposing they had promised her to get them solely from Mr Pickwick Sam's revelation of this, in open court, and its reception with laughter, showed what was thought of it. So which of the two courses were they to adopt? (3) And 'the proof we may get together about the whole conduct of the suit'. This 'whole conduct' was perfectly regular. So the judge thought – so did the jury. The case was proved by Pickwick's own friends. As we know, however, the firm took no steps to obtain satisfaction, but there cannot be the slightest doubt that they would have 'recovered damages'. We doubt if Mr Pickwick would have gone to the Fleet for the second time rather than pay.

Perker's suspicions as to the cognovit obtained by Dodson and Fogg were shrewd, and certain enough, though he could not have seen the document. The suspicions were well warranted by the state of the law, which became an instrument in the hands of grasping attorneys. By it the client was made to sign an acknowledgment, and offering no defence to a supposed action – say for costs – brought against him, judgment was then marked.

This offered a great temptation to the unscrupulous. Mrs Bardell, no doubt, signed with light heart, not knowing what she was doing, and being told that it was merely a matter of form. Various enactments attempted to protect the client – one being passed some four or five years before the trial Bardell v. Pickwick, requiring the cognovit to be regularly filed within twenty-one days; more than ten years later it was required that the client's signing such a thing should have no force in law, unless he was represented by another solicitor.

The matter, as we know, was compromised with Dodson and Fogg, so there was no need to scrutinize the cognovit. No doubt Perker was enabled to put pressure on the firm by hinting at such proceedings.

The damages, £750, were certainly moderate, and would not have been reduced by the court on an application to set them aside as 'excessive'. The good woman was quite at her ease, being no doubt certain that Mr Pickwick, at last, must give in. She could even enjoy the society of her friends and make the celebrated junketting to the 'Spaniards'. The firm took another view and grew tired of waiting; or they were sagacious enough to see that the arrest of their client was about the best method of putting pressure on Mr Pickwick. In this connection, it may be noted that Jackson's overzeal in the transaction might have led to an action against his employers; for he arrested not only Mrs Bardell, but her friends, Mrs Sanders and Mrs Cluppins. The prison gates were actually shut on them. 'Safe and sound,' said the Bailiff. 'Here we are at last,' said Jackson, 'all right and tight.'

True, Mrs Bardell put under her hand in her appealing letter to Mr Pickwick, that 'this business was from the very first fomented and encouraged and brought about by these men', but this is not much; for the view only occurs to her when her operations had completely failed and recoiled on her own head with such disastrous result. The firm's business was to persuade her that she had a good case, and the jury's verdict proved that she had. Had Mr Pickwick given in and paid, she would have had no scruples. One cannot, at the same time, but admire the ingenuity of the author, in bringing such a Nemesis on her. Dodson and Fogg, we are told, 'continue in business from which they realise a large income, and in which they are universally considered among the sharpest of the sharp'.

At the last interview, at Perker's, when the costs were paid, one might have expected Mr Pickwick to behave with a certain disdainful dignity. He was beaten and had paid over the stakes, and could afford to treat his enemy with contempt. Not so. The partners held out the olive branch by alluding to the way they had passed by his unmannerly attacks on them. 'I beg to assure you, sir, I bear you no ill will or vindictive feeling for sentiments you thought proper to express of us in our office,' and the other partner said, 'I hope you don't think quite so ill of us, etc.' This was rather gentlemanly and becoming. One offered his hand. But Mr Pickwick broke out in a perfect fury. They had assumed a tone of forgiveness which was 'an excess of impudence'. He had been 'the victim of their plots and conspiracies'. They had imprisoned and robbed him. It was 'insolent familiarity'. At last he said, '*You are a well-matched pair of mean, rascally, pettifogging robbers.*' This sentence he repeated three times, and the words 'Robbers' he shouted after them many times over the stairs.

Sharping attorneys! Why, a real sharping firm would have forced from their client advances of fee, 'cash out of pocket', have made her give a bill of sale on her lease and goods, and have fairly stripped her of everything before the case began. Of the damages – had they got them – she would have seen but little.

The cognovit that was extracted from Mrs Bardell was an acknowledgment, as we have seen, which entitled them to enter up judgment just as if a trial had taken place. In the Oxford great Dictionary, it reads quaintly to find Mrs Bardell's cognovit quoted as an illustration of the legal meaning.

The turnkey, on her arrest, had told Sam that she had been brought to the Fleet, 'on a cognovit for costs' Sam imparted this news to Job Trotter, and sent him off, hot foot, to Perker in Montague Place. This outcast was able to tell him, 'it seems they got a *cognovit* out of her for the amount of the costs, directly after the trial!'

Boz, on this occasion, gives us a happy glimpse of solicitor life.

Mr Perker had a dinner party that day, which was certified by the lights in the drawing-room windows, the sound of an improved grand piano, and an improveable cabinet voice issuing therefrom; and a rather overpowering smell of meat which pervaded the steps and entry. In fact, a couple of very good country agencies happening to come up to town at the same time, an agreeable little party had been got together to meet them, comprising Mr Snicks the Life Office Secretary, Mr Prosee the eminent counsel, three solicitors, one commissioner of bankrupts, a special pleader from the Temple, a small-eyed peremptory young gentleman, his pupil, who had written a lively book about the law of demises, with a vast quantity of marginal notes and references; and several other eminent and distinguished personages. From this society little Mr Perker detached himself on his clerk being announced in a whisper; and repairing to the dining-room, there found Mr Lowten and Job Trotter looking very dim and shadowy by the light of a kitchen candle, which the gentleman who condescended to appear in plush shorts and cottons for a quarterly stipend, had, with a becoming contempt for the clerk and all things appertaining to 'the office', placed upon the table.

'Now, Lowten,' said little Mr Perker, shutting the door, 'what's the matter? No important letter come in a parcel, is there?'

Do we not seem to be present? We can never pass by Russell Square without calling up the scene. Note, too, the components of that legal dinner. Poor Sir F. Lockwood used to declare that he relished 'Mr Prosee, the eminent counsel' more than any one of Boz's legal circle. Yet these five words are all we know of him. But Sir Frank had imagination, and like some of us could read between the lines, or rather, between the words. Here was a prominent member of the Bar – was he K.C.? a triton among the minnows – therefore heading the table, listened to with reverence as he told of the judges, possibly of 'old Stareleigh's' last exhibition of petulance – 'with it's high time for him to go, etc.' But if he had not silk, why did not Perker retain him instead of the incapable Phunky, whom he did not ask on this occasion. 'I gave the chap a good chance, but he destroyed my whole case!' 'Catch me letting him put his legs under my mahogany.' Among the guests was that 'small-eyed, peremptory young gentleman' – the special pleader's pupil. What a capital sketch has Boz given of him. 'He had written a lively book about the law of demises, with a vast quantity of marginal notes and references.' He had come with his teacher, who was no doubt highly deferential to Mr Prosee, but enough, the peremptory young gentleman may have partly 'tackled' the great man on some point of practice. The good country agencies must have gone home delighted with their evening.

But Mr Prosee may be brought into somewhat closer communication with the case. At Perker's dinner the gentlemen had gone up to the drawing room, when Perker was called down to hear the news of Mrs Bardell's arrest. Mr Prosee was left expatiating to the circle on some beautiful 'point', and when Perker returned how likely that he should tell of his extraordinary client who had preferred to go to prison rather than pay the costs of a suit, 'And here,' he would go on, 'is the drollest sequel you ever heard, etc.'

'An odd unusual thing,' Mr Prosee would say. 'Plaintiff and defendant, both in jail together! I never heard the like.' There would be much laughter at the novel situation. Thus the cognovit would come up and Mr Prosee gravely say, 'Nothing will be done till an Act of Parliament is passed. The client should be protected by a fresh solicitor.' On which the young author of the treatise on demises would have something to say in his best fashion; for the cognovit might be taken to be a sort of demise. 'I doubt, Mr Prosee, if your suggestion would work. As I take it, sir, etc.'

But the circumstances connected with Mr Pickwick's release from the Fleet, show the adroitness and ability of Dodson in a high degree. It will be recollected that when Job rushed with the news to Perker, that gentleman and his clerk broke out into rapturous admiration.

'Now, Lowten,' said little Mr Perker, shutting the door, 'what's the matter? No important letter come in a parcel, is there?'

'No, sir,' replied Lowten. 'This is a messenger from Mr Pickwick, sir.'

'From Pickwick, eh?' said the little man, turning quickly to Job. 'Well; what is it?'

'Dodson and Fogg have taken Mrs Bardell in execution for her costs, sir,' said Job.

'No!' exclaimed Perker, putting his hands in his pockets, and reclining against the sideboard.

'Yes,' said Job. 'It seems they got a cognovit out of her for the amount of 'em, directly after the trial.'

'By Jove!' said Perker, taking both hands out of his pockets and striking the knuckles of his right against the palm of his left, emphatically, 'those are the cleverest scamps I ever had anything to do with!'

'The sharpest practitioners *I* ever knew, sir,' observed Lowten.

'Sharp!' echoed Perker. 'There's no knowing where to have them.'

'Very true, sir, there is not,' replied Lowten; and then both master and man pondered for a few seconds, with animated countenances, as if they were reflecting upon one of the most beautiful and ingenious discoveries that the intellect of man had ever made. When they had in some measure recovered from their trance of admiration, Job Trotter discharged himself of the rest of his commission. Perker nodded his head thoughtfully, and pulled out his watch.

Now to the superficial this seemed to be evaded by the art of the firm in 'getting the cognovit out of her'. But this was an ordinary, vulgar stroke – which anyone could have done. Their policy went far deeper, and this Perker was acute enough to recognise. There was no object in putting Mrs Bardell into the Fleet.

They could no more get their costs out of her, than they could get them out of Mr Pickwick. She had nothing but her few 'sticks' of furniture, worth say £50. But the astute fellows saw what pressure could be put on the benevolent nature of Mr Pickwick, who could not endure that a respectable woman should be exposed to the contamination of a debtor's prison. And their sagacity was to be justified, and on the very next day, too.

It is curious, however, that no mention is made of Mrs Bardell's release. It, of course, took place before Mr Pickwick's. Here again Dodson and Fogg behaved very fairly, for they allowed both her and Mr Pickwick to be released, without receiving payment, but simply on 'an understanding' by Perker. As it turned out, indeed, they were not paid for some weeks.

The processes by which Mr Pickwick was got into the Fleet were complicated enough, *Habeas Corpus*, appearing before functionaries, etc. But it is odd that in cases of persons of lower degree these seemed not to be necessary. We do not hear of them in Sam's instance. While Mrs Bardell was taken straight from 'the Spaniards', to the prison door, she was not even formally arrested by the Bailiff, though he was in attendance. He sat afar off at Hampstead, taking his drink – and on the box during the drive. She might be said to have been arbitrarily taken to the prison by Jackson – without a legal warrant. Had not the business been compromised, some other astute firm of attorneys might have found subject for an action against Dodson and Fogg.

Another of the humorous incidents connected with the case is old Weller's firm persuasion that Mr Pickwick was to 'stand his trial', as though he were indicted for some criminal offence. We find him always astray as to when he was to be 'tried', etc. This is a most natural impression among the lower classes, who are not very clear as to the distinction between civil and criminal process, being most familiar with the latter. In the same spirit is his humorous suggestion of securing an *alibi*, as the best method of getting Mr Pickwick off. 'O Sammy, Sammy, vy worn't there a allcybi!'

Such is 'The Trial in Pickwick'.

Is there any writer, now living, I may be asked, who could furnish such a picture as this, one so full of reality and true humour, of one of our modern courts of justice? The answer must be that it would be idle to look for such a person. There are thousands who could supply minute drawings in which not a single detail would be omitted. But the piercing to the essence, the happy generalization, the knowledge of the true points of character, these would be sought in vain.

BIOGRAPHICAL NOTE

Percy Hetherington Fitzgerald was born in 1834 in Ireland at Fane Valley, County Louth. He was educated at Stonyhurst College, Lancashire, and subsequently at Trinity College, Dublin. He was called to the Irish Bar and became a crown prosecutor on the northeastern circuit.

Having moved to London, Fitzgerald embarked on a career as a writer, beginning by writing fiction but quickly building himself a reputation as an author of works of history and philosophy. A personal friend of Charles Dickens, he became a contributor to Dickens' magazine, *Household Words*, and later dramatic critic for the *Observer* and the *Whitehall Review*. He was also an accomplished sculptor and artist.

Fitzgerald died in 1925 and, following a requiem in Westminster Cathedral, is buried in Glasnevin Cemetery in Dublin.

HESPERUS PRESS

Hesperus Press is committed to bringing near what is far – far both in space and time. Works written by the greatest authors, and unjustly neglected or simply little known in the English-speaking world, are made accessible through new translations and a completely fresh editorial approach. Through these classic works, the reader is introduced to the greatest writers from all times and all cultures.

For more information on Hesperus Press, please visit our website: **www.hesperuspress.com**